AF604556
Hello, my name is Marlee.
About me
My name is ______________________.

Track your progress

Find and trace each letter to match your completed pages.

a s o c g k e u w v x y z

x as in "wax"

Teacher note As each letter page is completed, students trace the letter on this tracker.

t
p
i
d
m
n
r
h
b
j
l
f
q
I'm hiding ... circle me when you find me on the pages.

Before you begin writing …

Posture

- Relax your arms
- Sit back in your chair
- Make sure your back is straight.

Put your feet flat on the floor.

Pencil grip

How you hold your pencil is important.

- Hold your pencil firmly between your thumb and index finger.
- Balance the pencil on your middle finger.
- Don't grip the pencil too tightly!

Left-handed Right-handed

Paper position

- Tilt your page.
- Use your non-writing hand to steady the paper.

Left-handed

Right-handed

Numbers

Teacher note

Correct number formation is essential in mathematics and should be as fluent and automatic as handwriting letters and words.

Warm-up patterns

Teacher note *Trace these patterns in different colours.*

Track Trace Copy

Track

Trace

Copy

Self-assessment!

Ask students to circle their best lower-case s and upper-case S. Ask them to explain their reasons to you or a classmate.

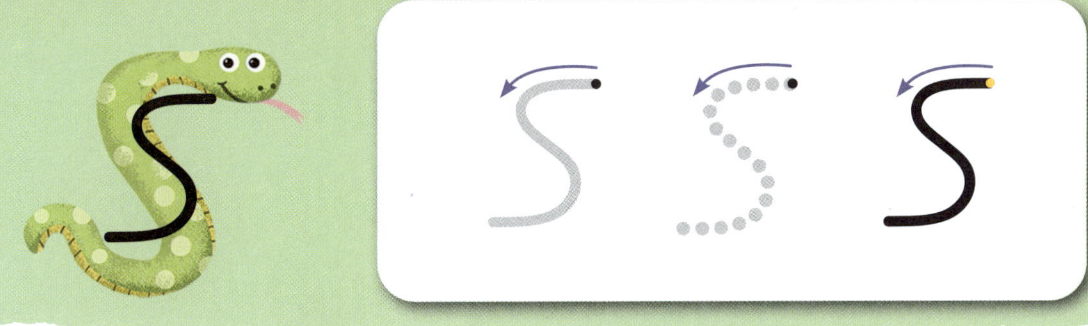

above

on

below

above

on

below

above

on

below

above

on

below

Fast finishers Colour in the picture of the Sun, and then draw something else that begins with the /s/ phoneme (sound), for example, socks or a snake.

Track

Trace

Copy

Self-assessment! Ask students to circle their best lower-case a and upper-case A. Ask them to explain the reason for their choices to you or a classmate.

above
A
on
below
above
A
on
below
above
a
on
below
above
a
on
below

Fast finishers Trace over the letter a, and then colour in the picture of the ant.

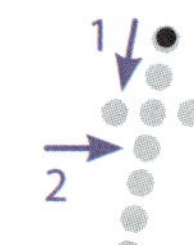

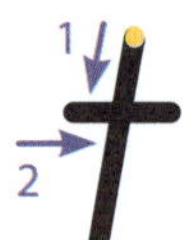

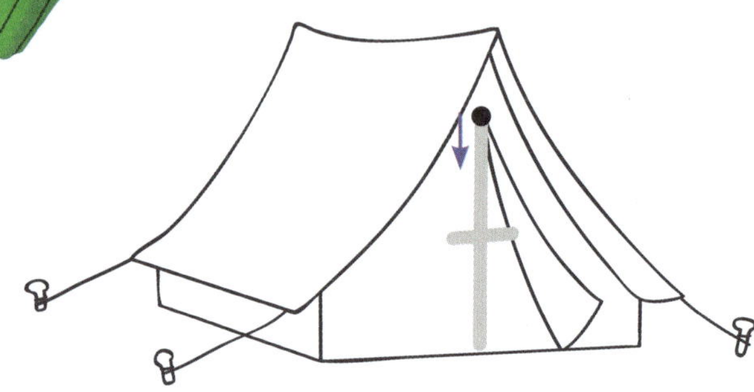

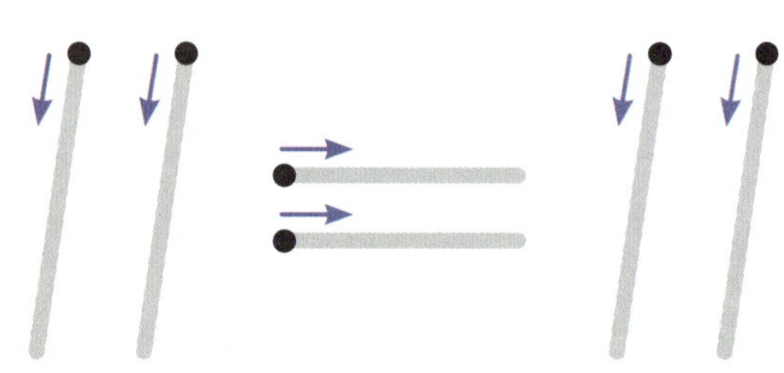

Track

Trace

Copy

Self-assessment!

Ask students to circle their best lower-case t and upper-case T.
Ask them to explain the reason for their choices to you or a classmate.

OXFORD UNIVERSITY PRESS

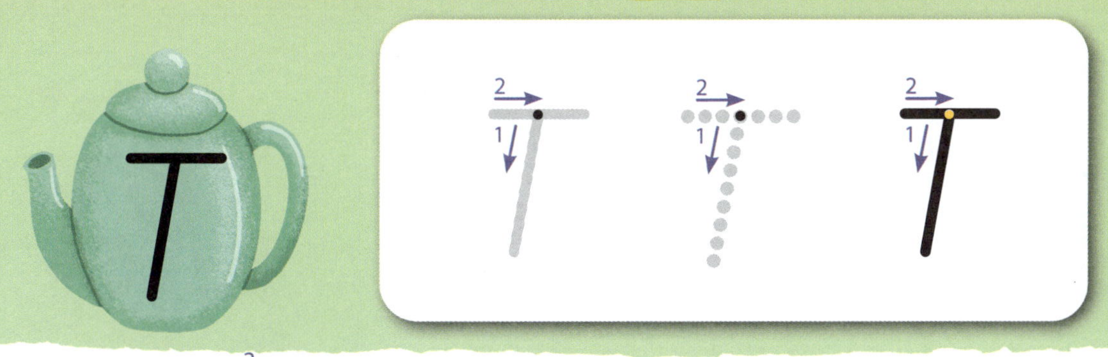

above
on
below
above
on
below
above
on
below
above
on
below

Fast finishers

Trace over the letter t, and then colour in this picture of a tap.

Track

Trace

Copy

Self-assessment!

Ask students to circle their best lower-case p and upper-case P. Ask them to explain the reason for their choices to you or a classmate.

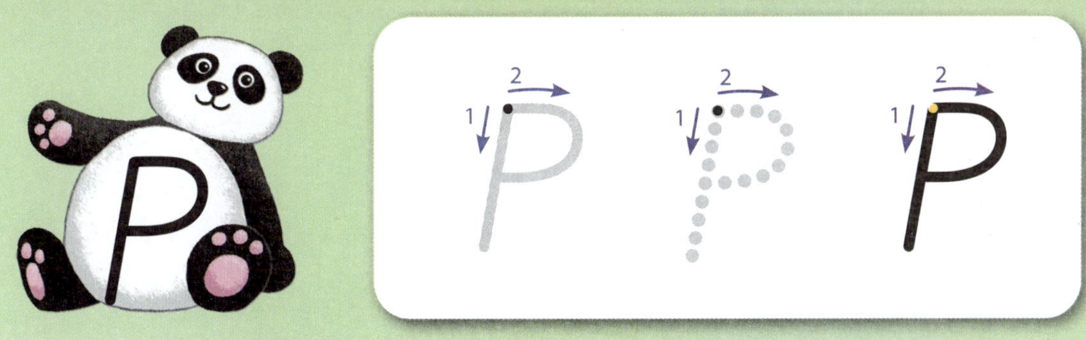

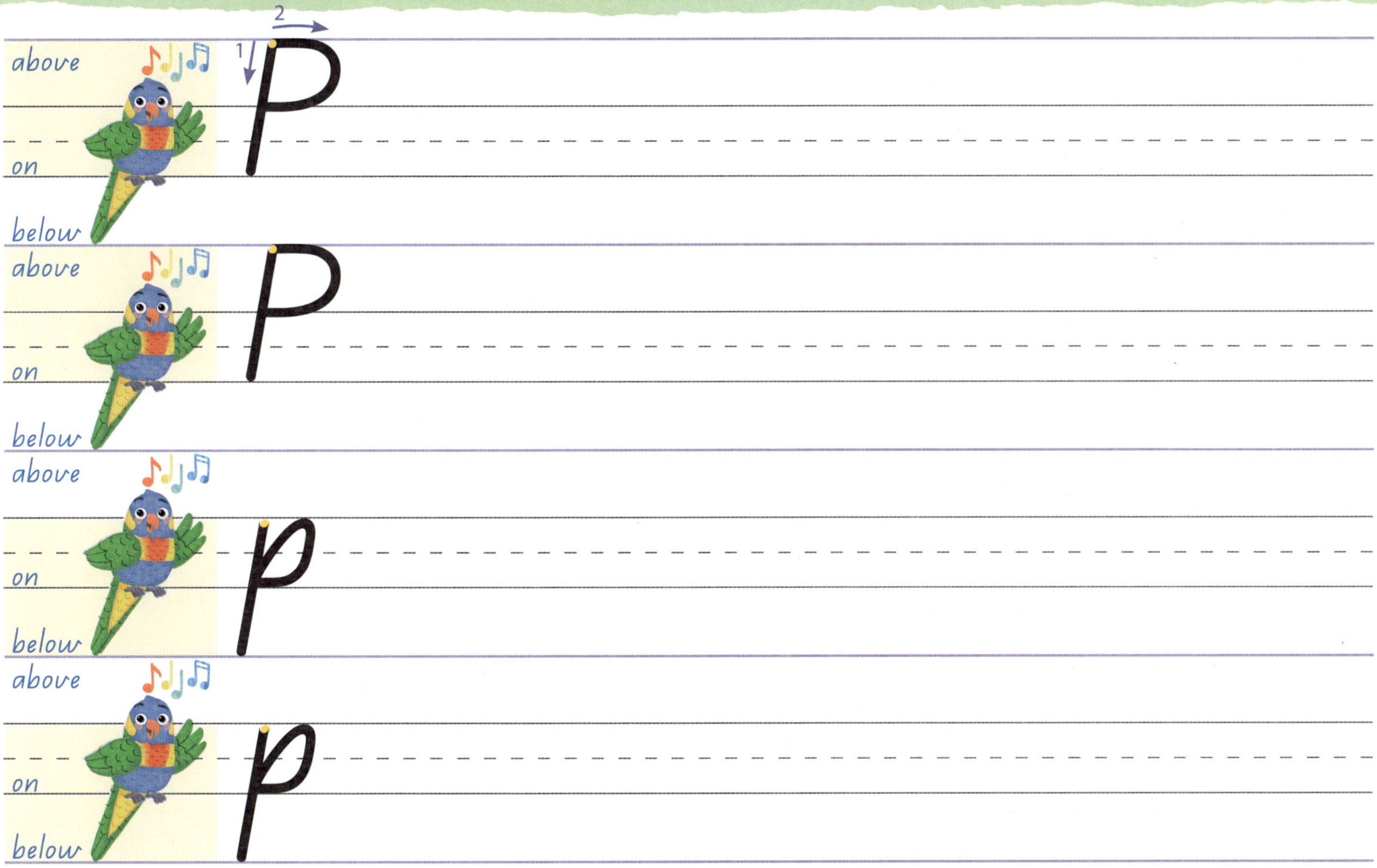

2
1
P

above
on
below

P

above
on
below

p

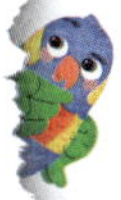

above
on
below

p

above
on
below

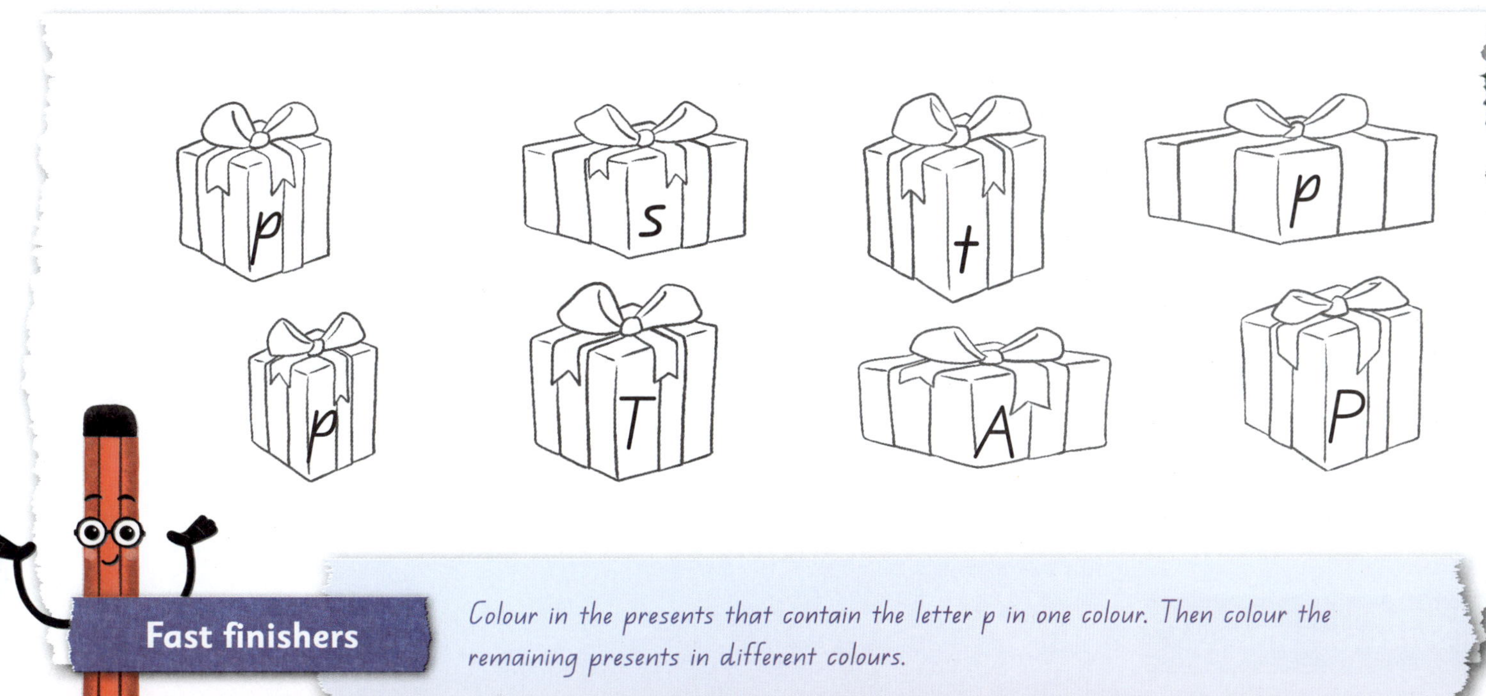

Fast finishers

Colour in the presents that contain the letter p in one colour. Then colour the remaining presents in different colours.

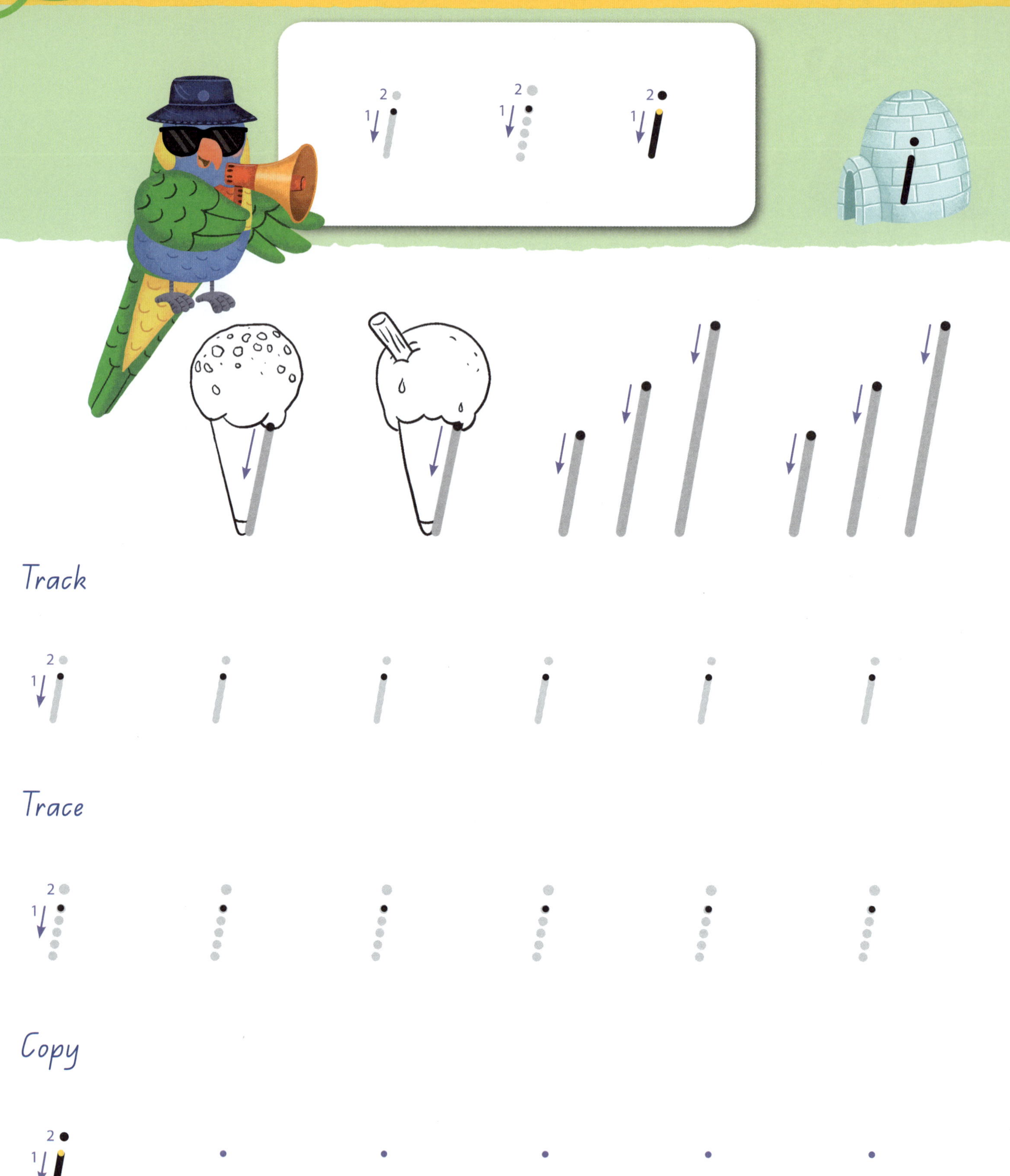

Track

Trace

Copy

Self-assessment!

Ask students to circle their best lower-case i and upper-case I.
Ask them to explain the reason for their choices to you or a classmate.

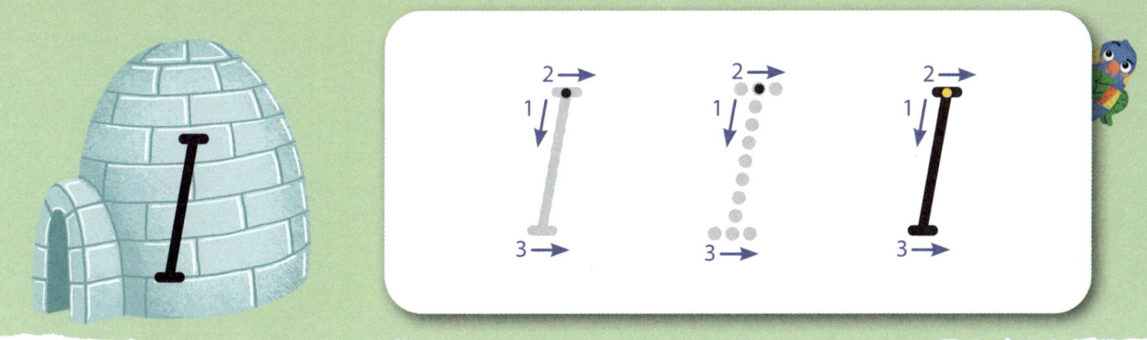

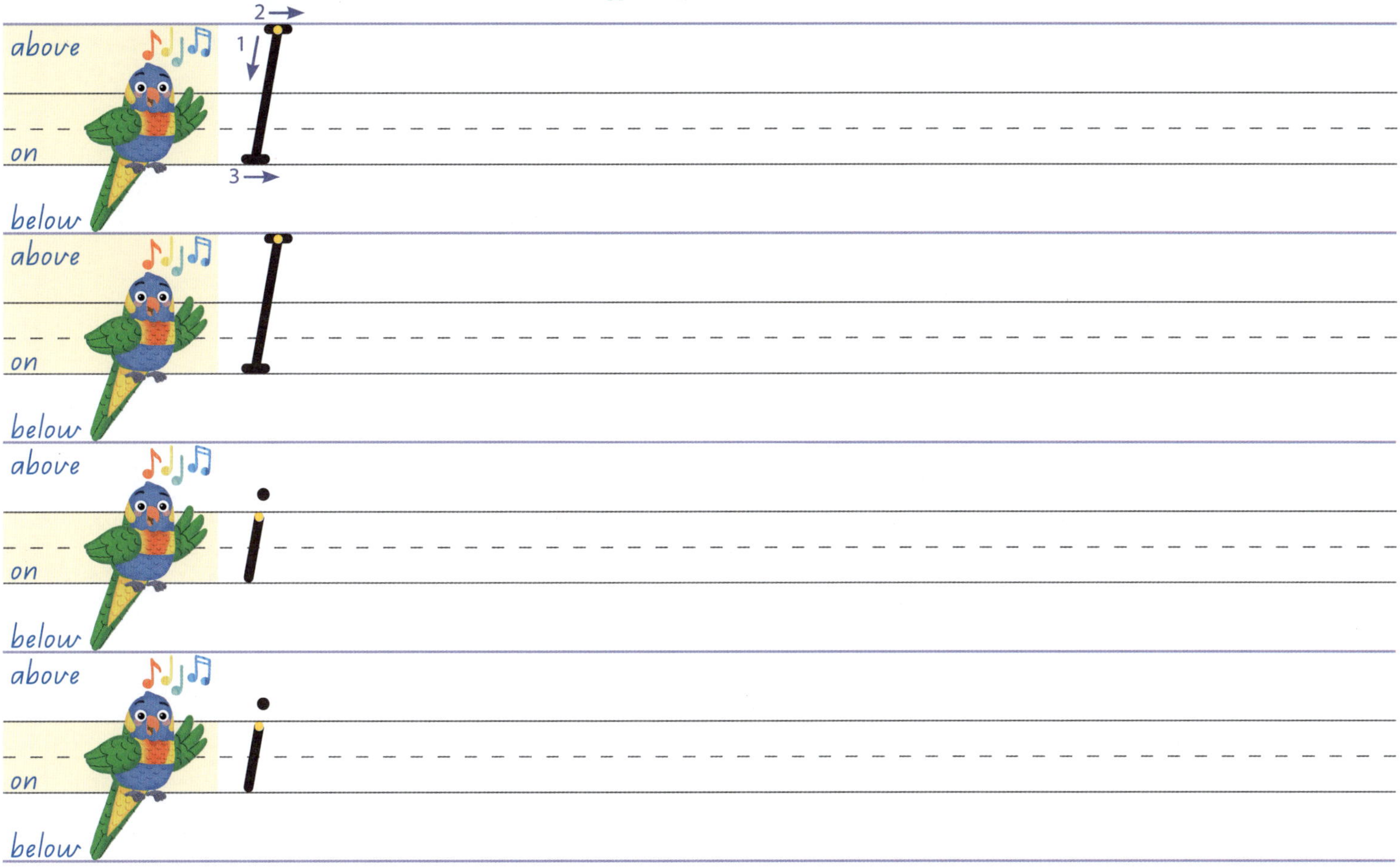

above
on
below

above
on
below

above
on
below

above
on
below

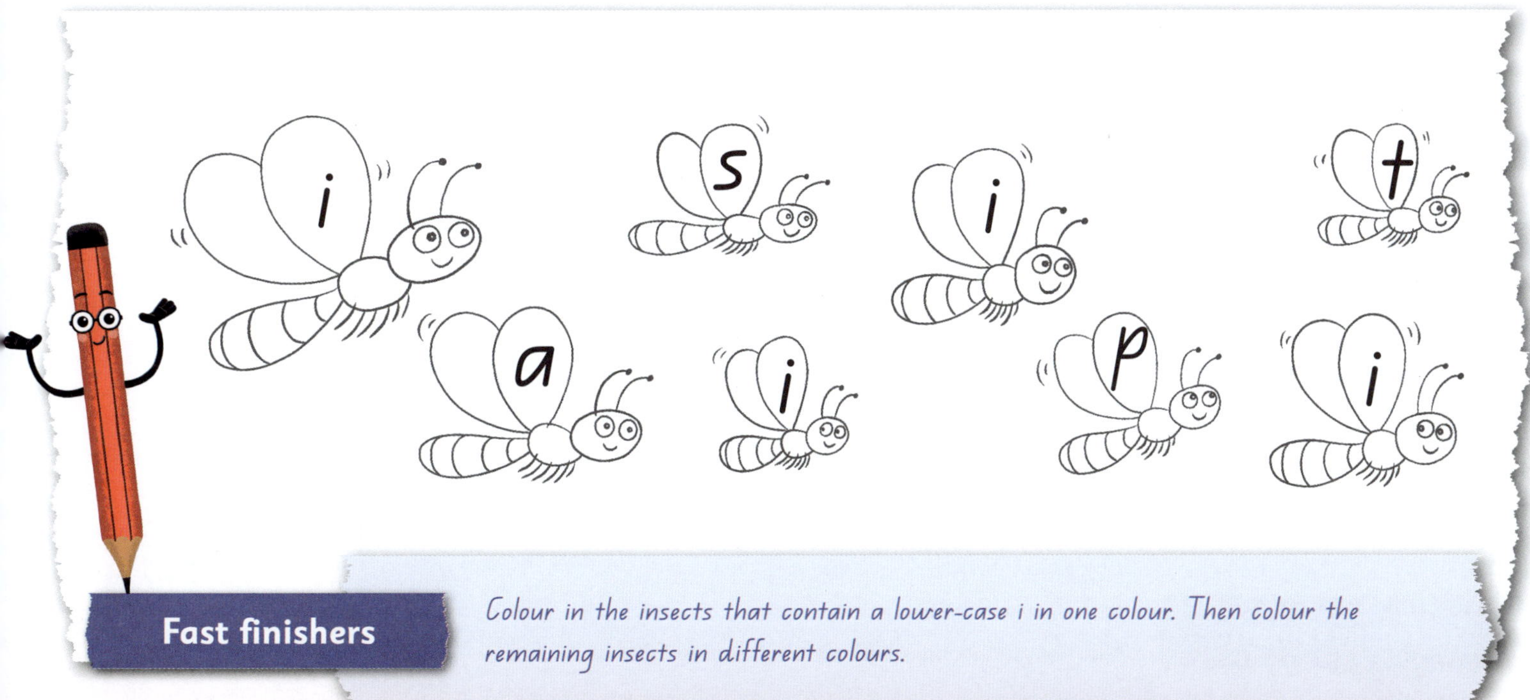

Fast finishers

Colour in the insects that contain a lower-case i in one colour. Then colour the remaining insects in different colours.

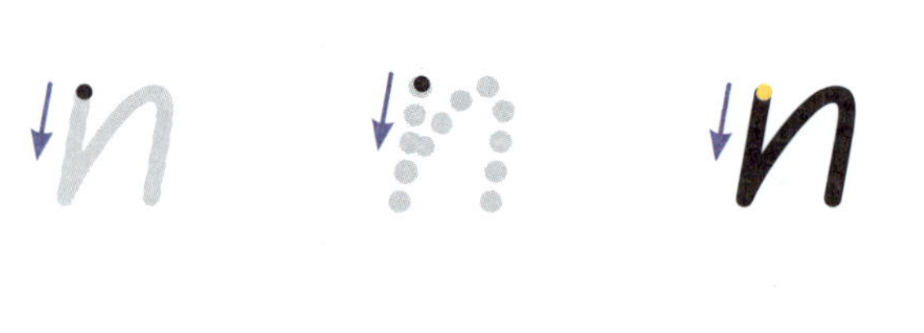

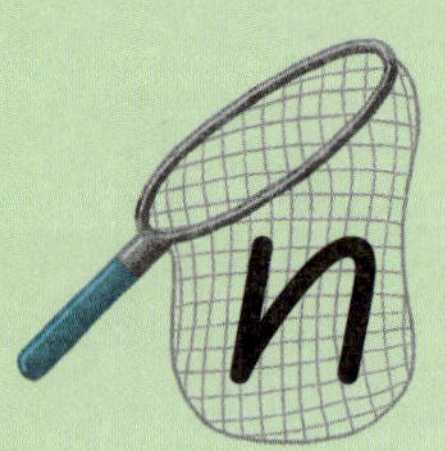

Track

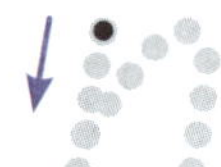      

Trace

Copy

Self-assessment!

Ask students to circle their best lower-case n and upper-case N.
Ask them to explain the reason for their choices to you or a classmate.

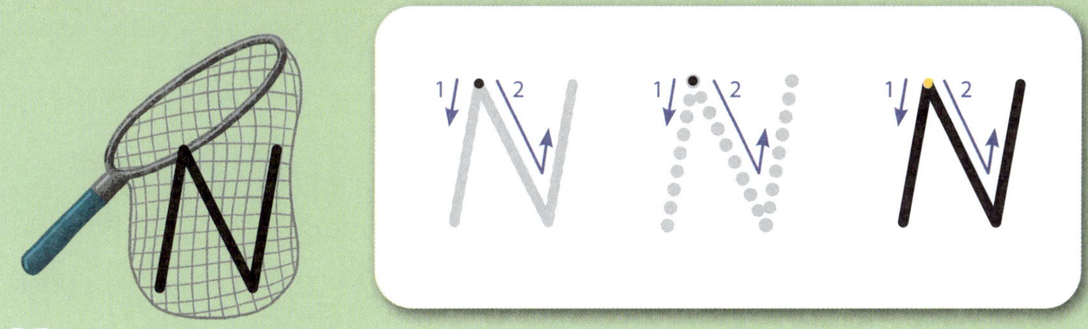

1 2 N

above
on
below

N

above
on
below

n

above
on
below

n

above
on
below

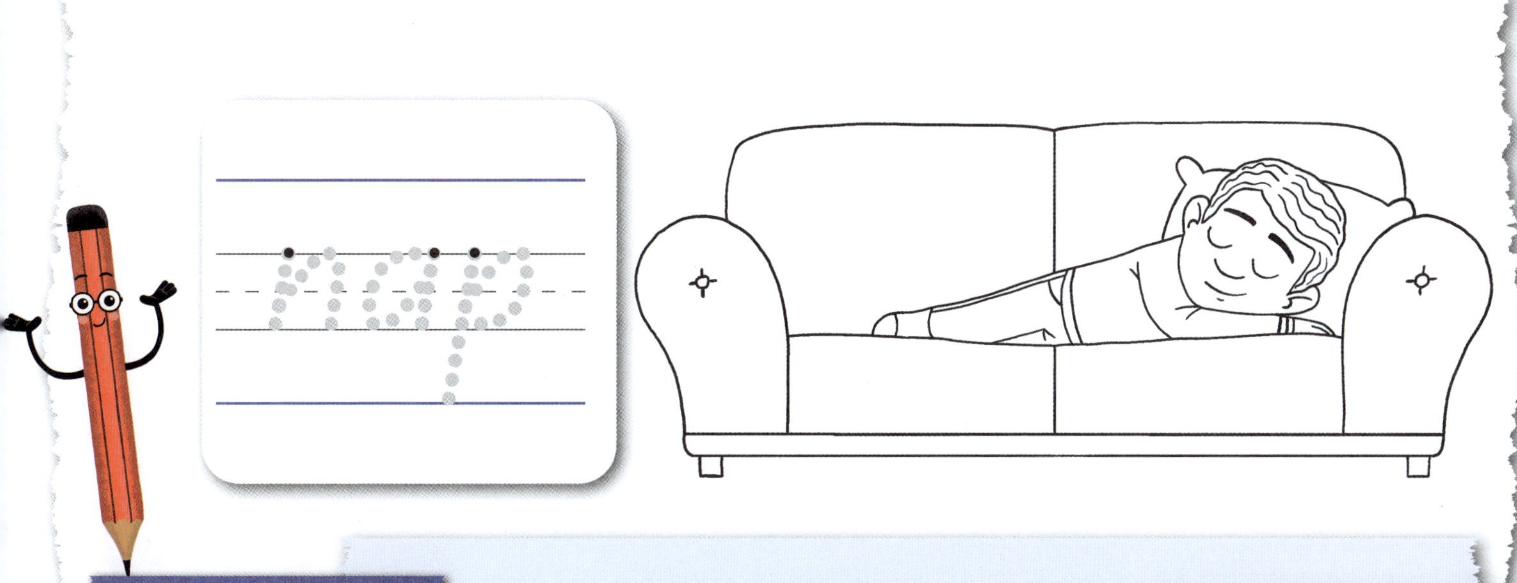

Fast finishers Trace over the word "nap", and then colour in the picture of the child having a nap.

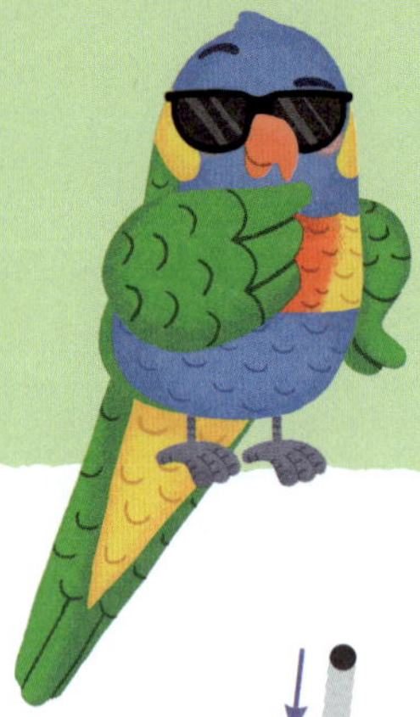

m m m

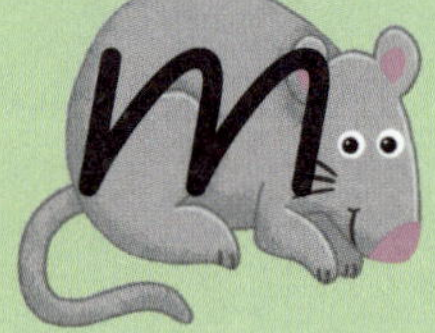

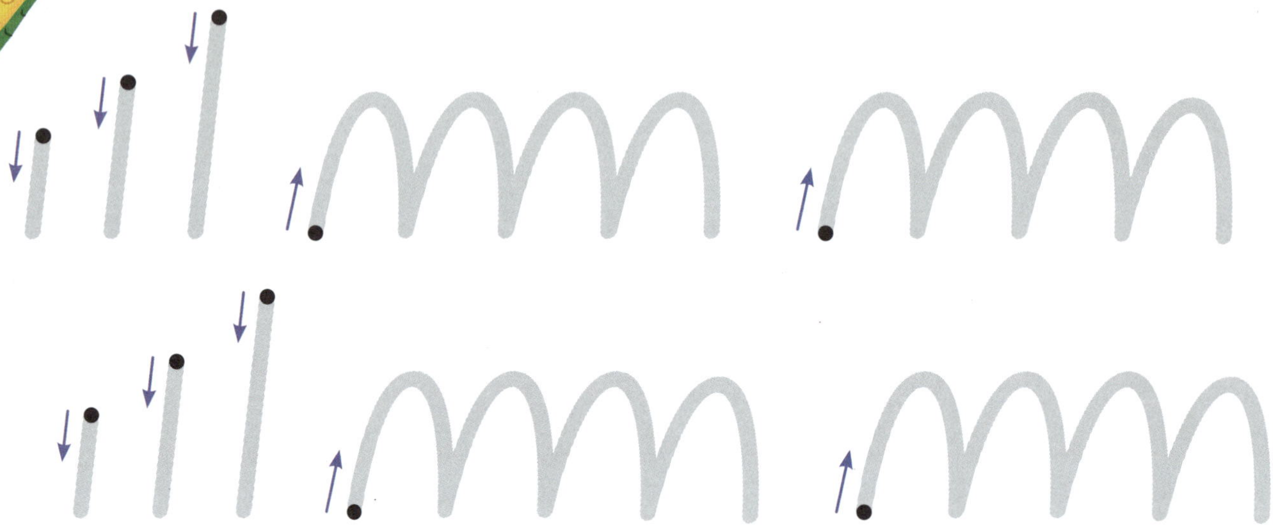

Track

Trace

Copy

Self-assessment!

Ask students to circle their best lower-case m and upper-case M. Ask them to explain the reason for their choices to you or a classmate.

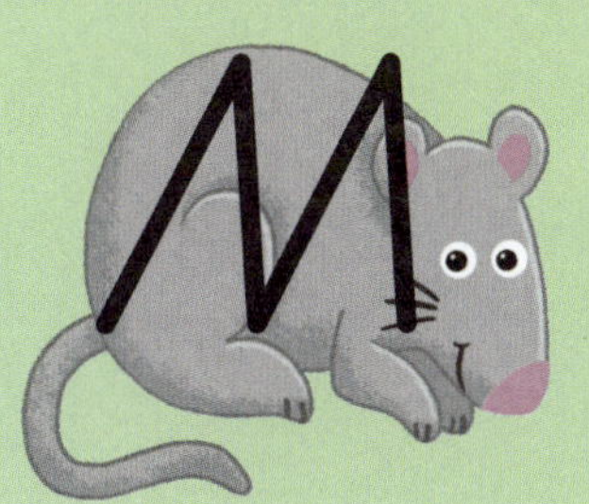

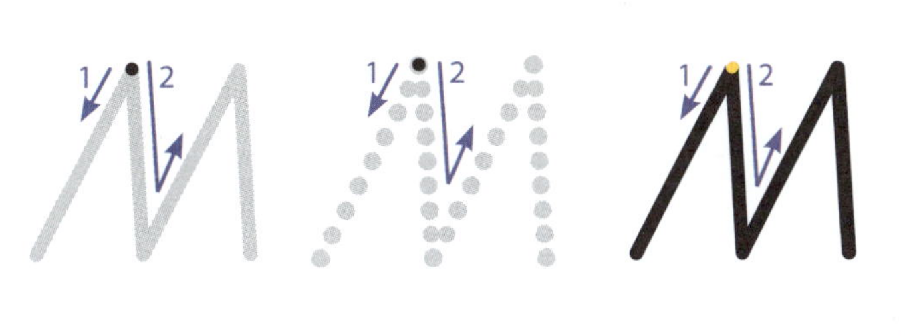

M M M

above

on

below

above

on

below

above

on

below

above

on

below

map

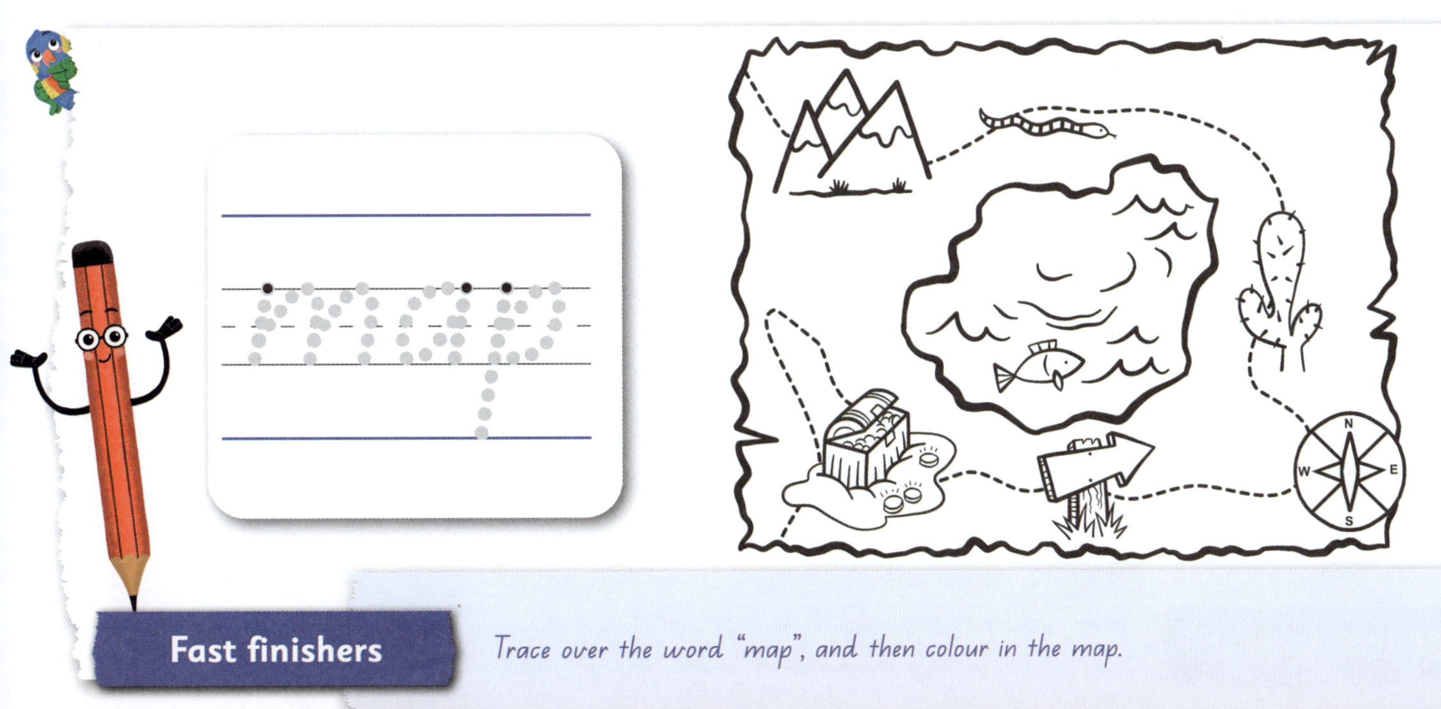

Fast finishers

Trace over the word "map", and then colour in the map.

Track

Trace

Copy

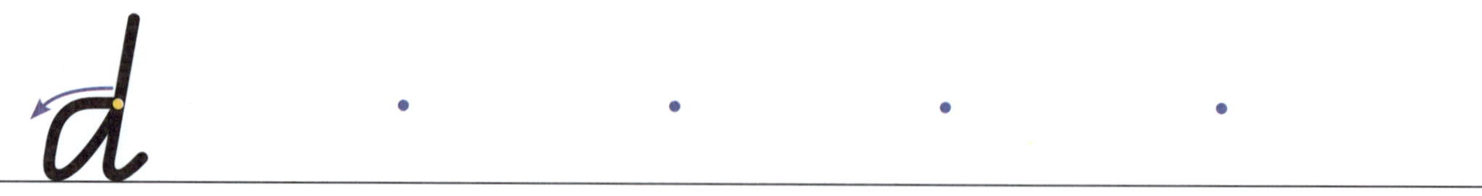

Self-assessment!

Ask students to circle their best lower-case d and upper-case D. Ask them to explain the reason for their choices to you or a classmate.

Fast finishers

Trace over the names, and then colour in the drawing of Sam and her dad.

Track

Trace

Copy

Self-assessment!

Ask students to circle their best lower-case g and upper-case G.
Ask them to explain the reason for their choices to you or a classmate.

above
on
below
G

above
on
below
G

above
on
below
g

above
on
below
g

Fast finishers

Colour in the flowerpots that contain a lower-case g in one colour. Then colour the remaining flowerpots and all the flowers in different colours.

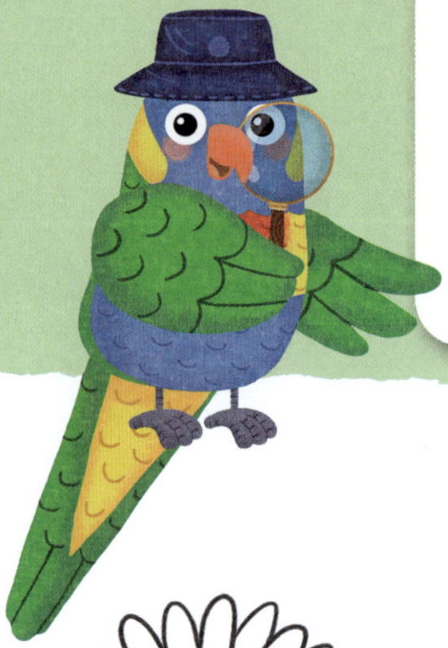

o o o

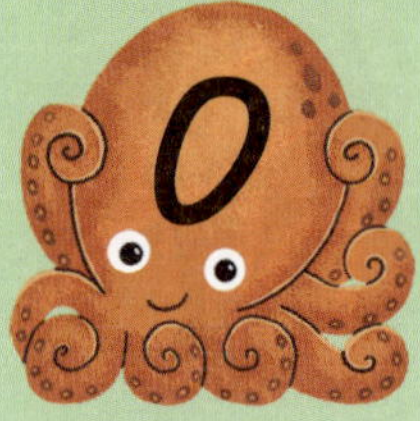

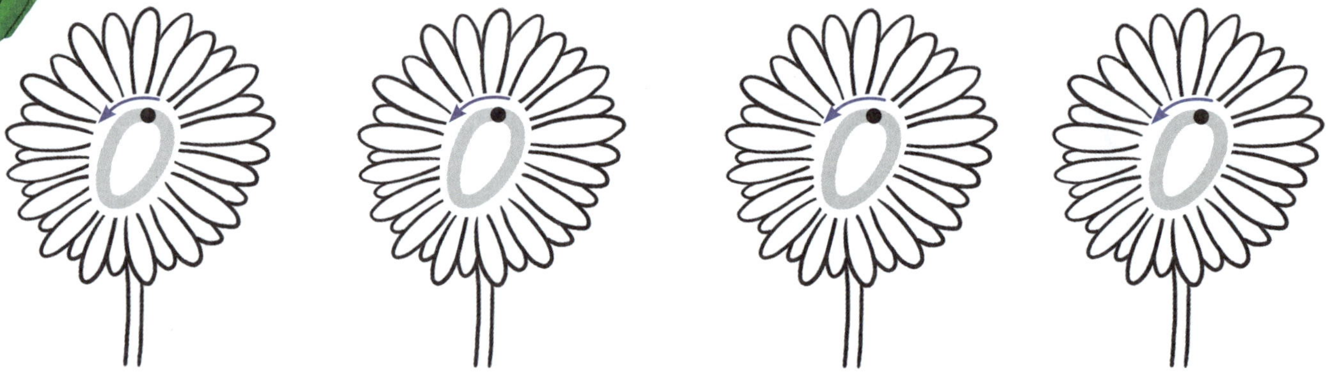

Track

o o o o o o

Trace

o o o o o o

Copy

o

Self-assessment!

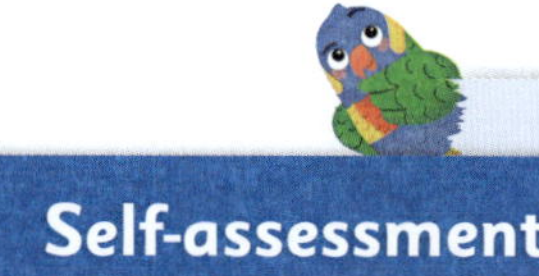

Ask students to circle their best lower-case o and upper-case O.
Ask them to explain the reason for their choices to you or a classmate.

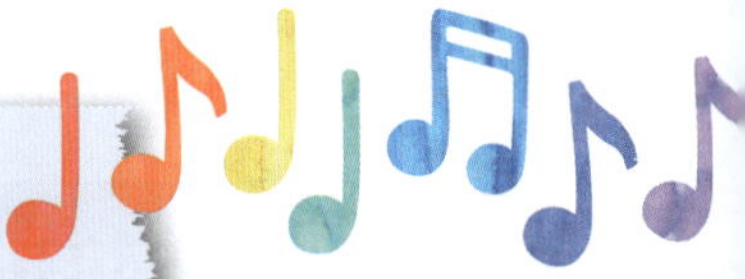

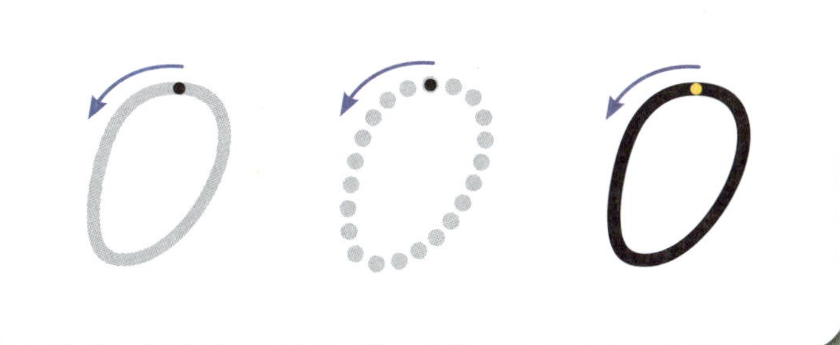

above
on
below
O

above
on
below
O

above
on
below
o

above
on
below
o

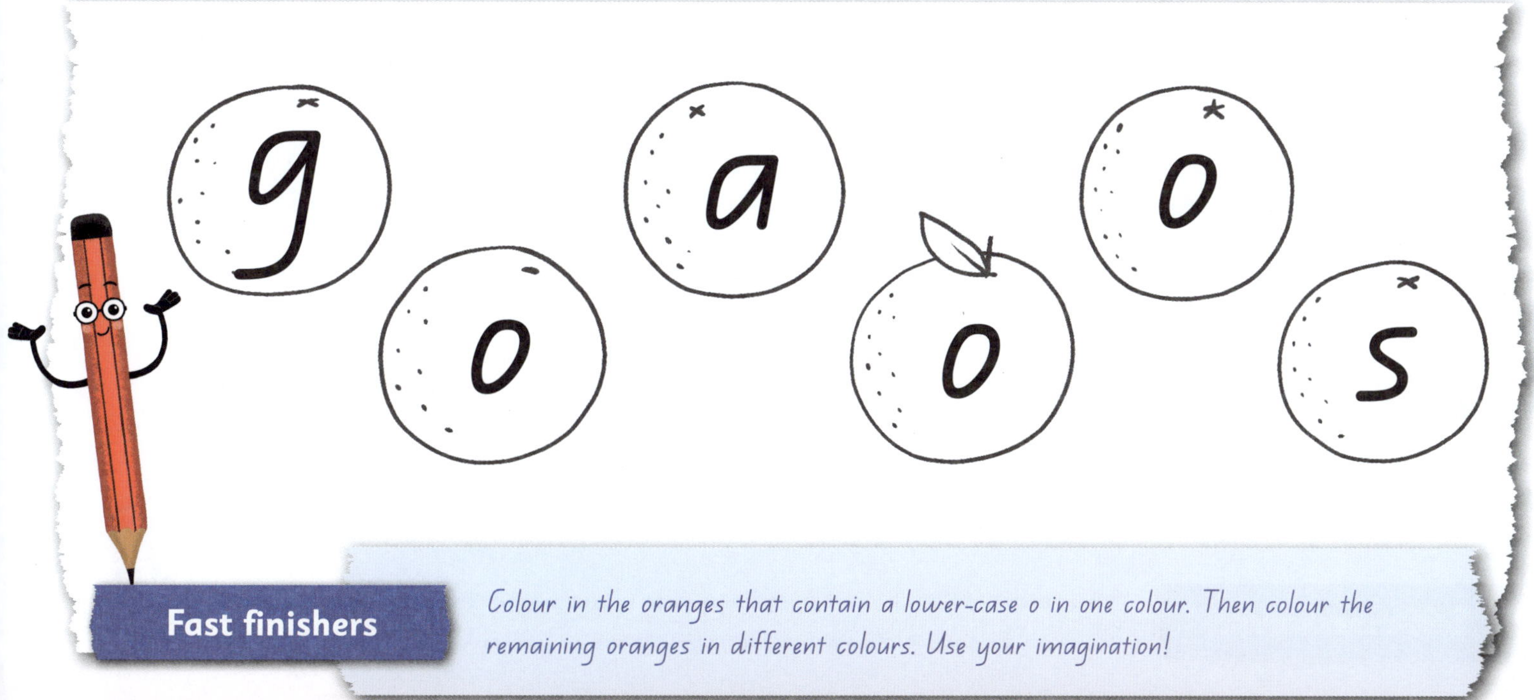

Fast finishers

Colour in the oranges that contain a lower-case o in one colour. Then colour the remaining oranges in different colours. Use your imagination!

Track

Trace

Copy

Self-assessment!

Ask students to circle their best lower-case c and upper-case C.
Ask them to explain the reason for their choices to you or a classmate.

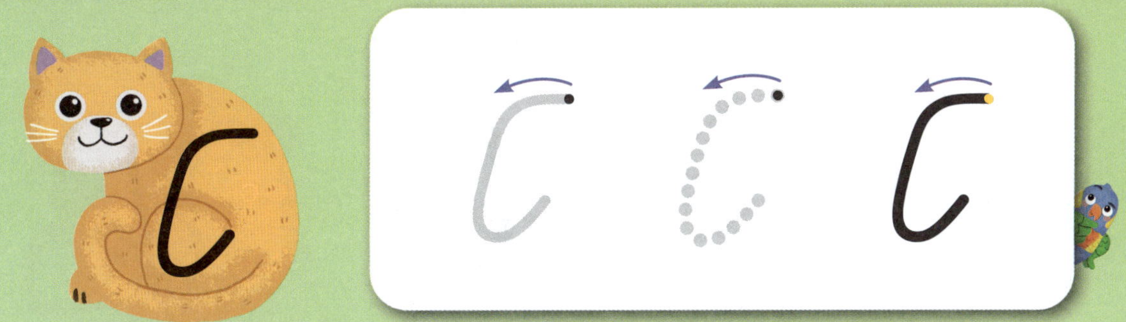

c c c

above
on
below
c

above
on
below
c

above
on
below
c

above
on
below
c

can

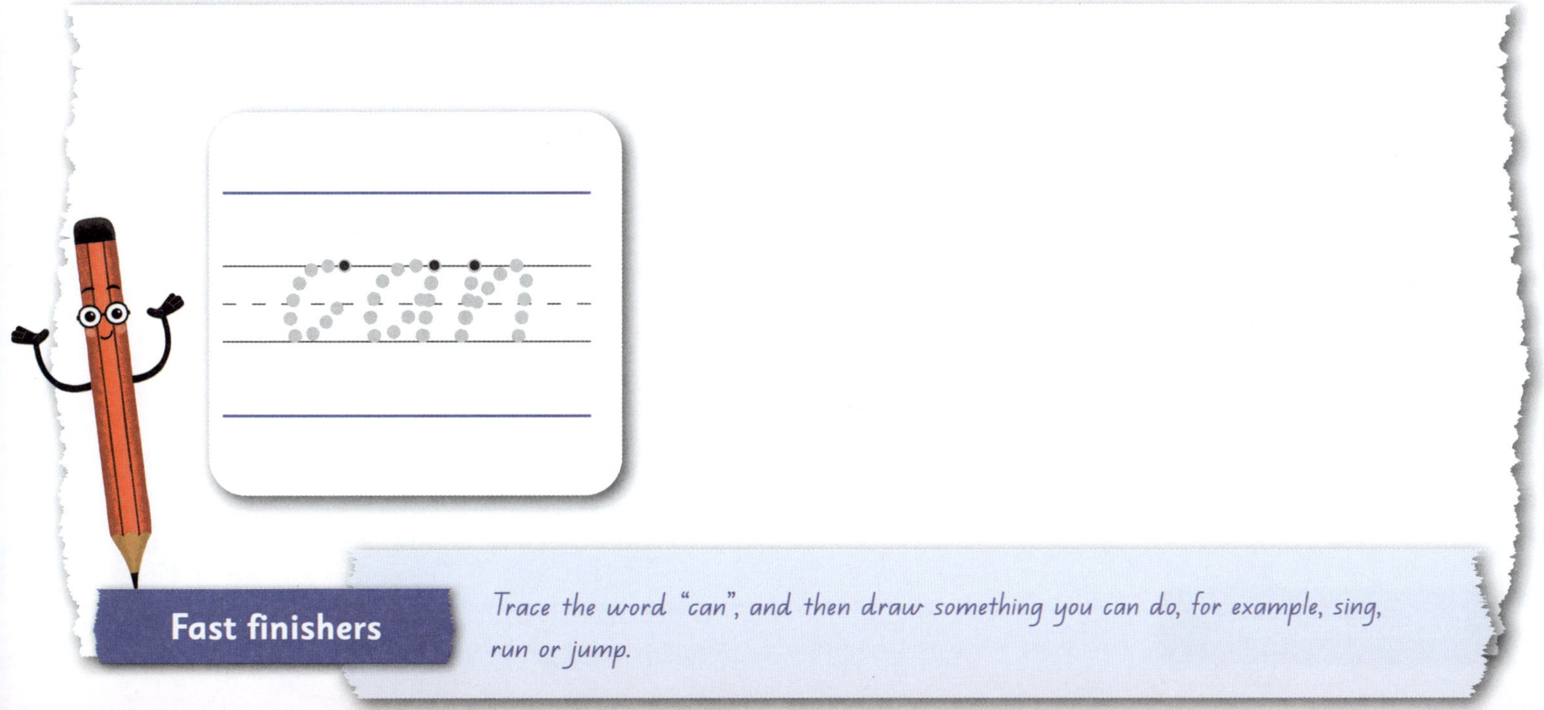

Fast finishers

Trace the word "can", and then draw something you can do, for example, sing, run or jump.

Self-assessment!

Ask students to circle their best lower-case k and upper-case K.
Ask them to explain the reason for their choices to you or a classmate.

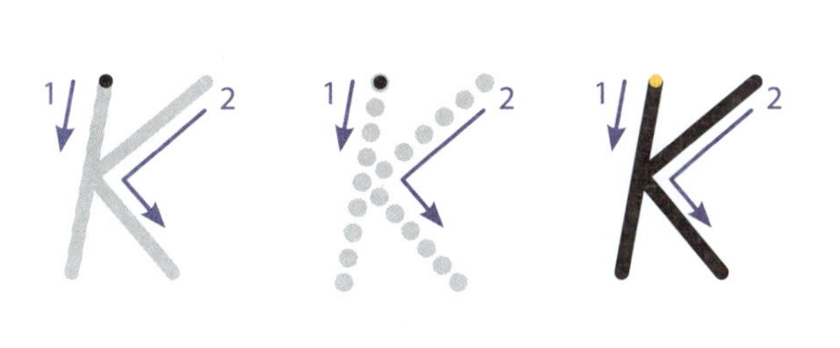

above
on 
below
K

above 
on
below
K

above 
on
below
k

above 
on
below
k

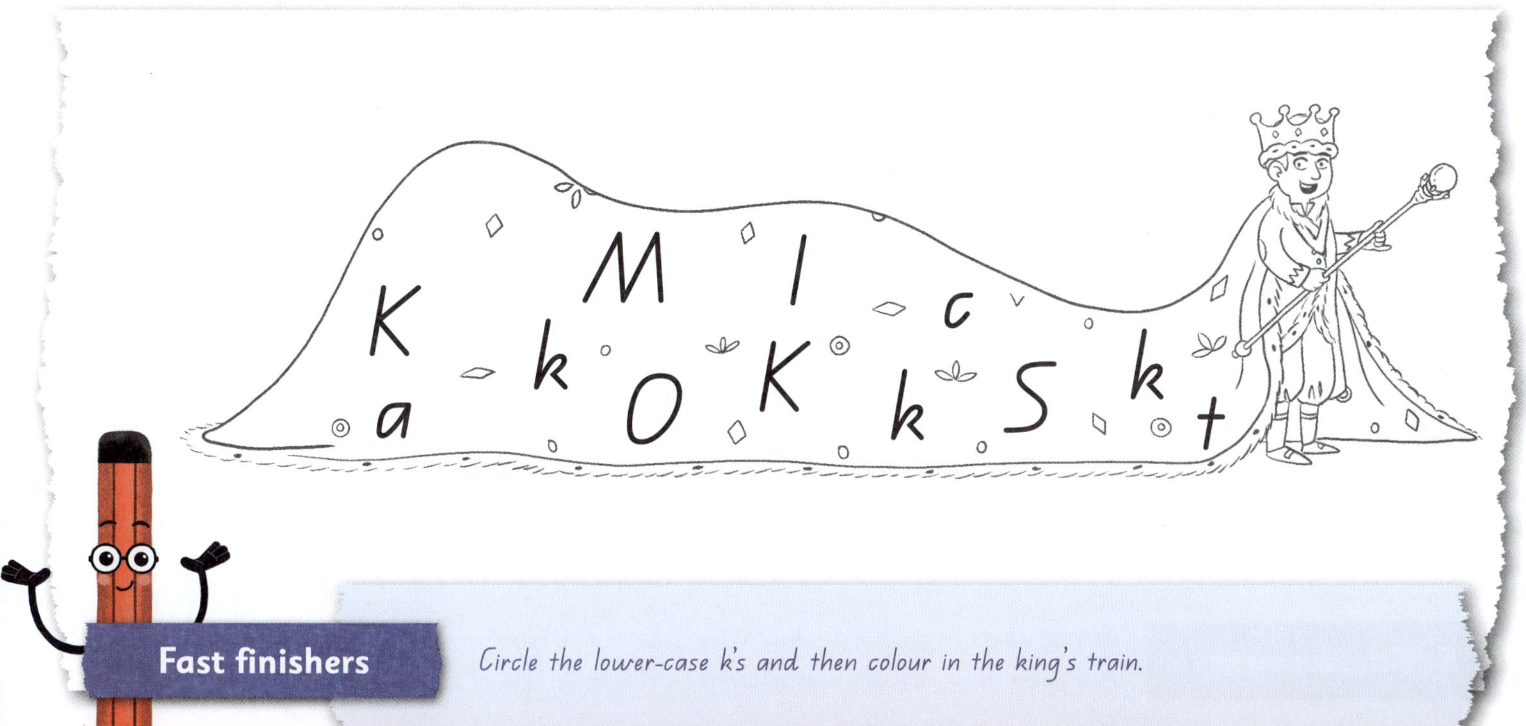

Fast finishers

Circle the lower-case k's and then colour in the king's train.

e e e

e

Track

Trace

Copy

Self-assessment!

Ask students to circle their best lower-case e and upper-case E. Ask them to explain the reason for their choices to you or a classmate.

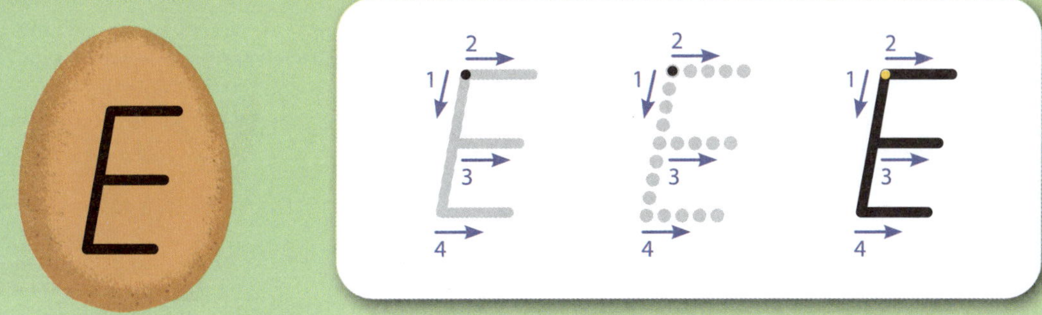

E E E

above
on
below
E

above
on
below
E

above
on
below
e

above
on
below
e

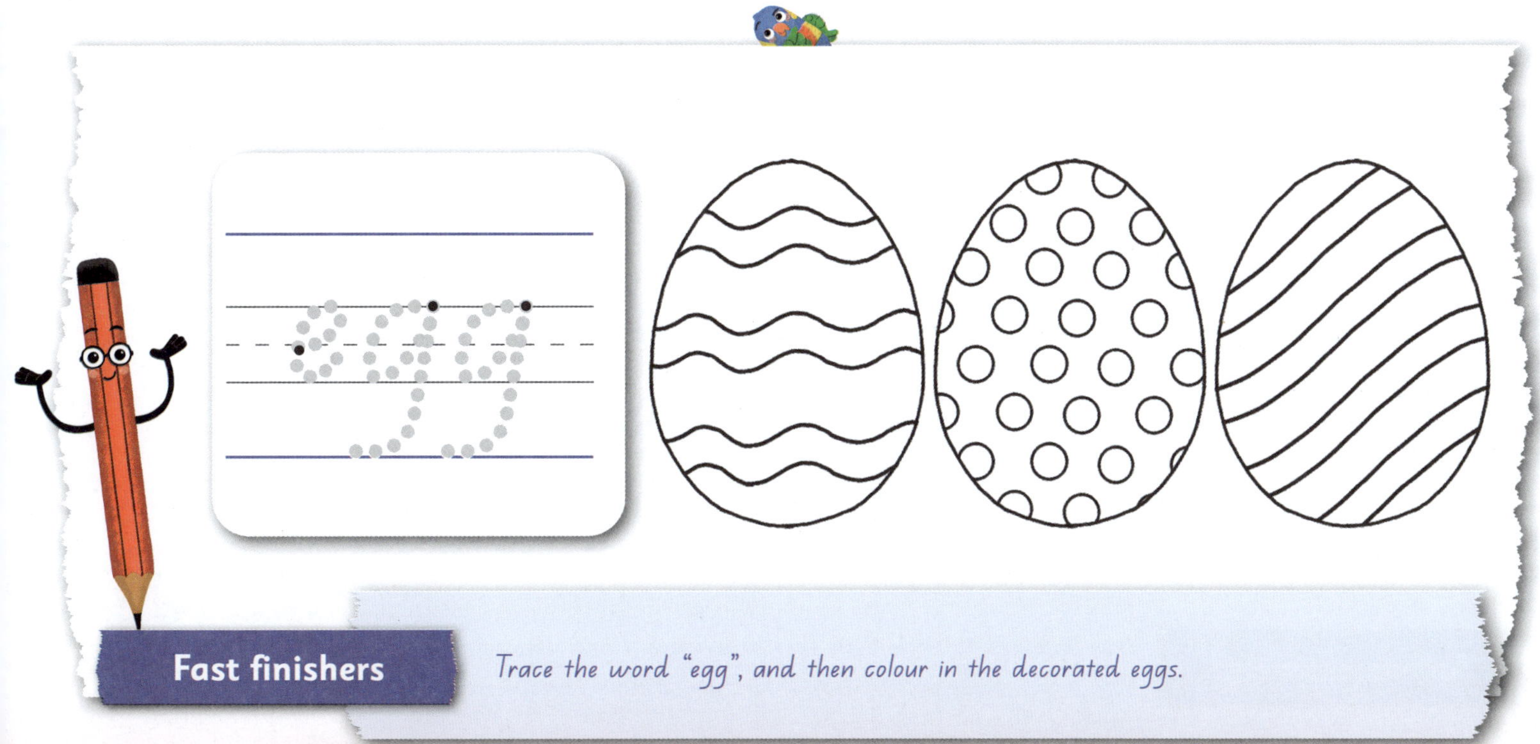

Fast finishers Trace the word "egg", and then colour in the decorated eggs.

u u u

u

uuuu uuuu uuuu uuuu uuuu

Track

u u u u u u

Trace

u u u u u u

Copy

u

Self-assessment!

Ask students to circle their best lower-case u and upper-case U. Ask them to explain the reason for their choices to you or a classmate.

above

on

below

above

on

below

above

on

below

above

on

below

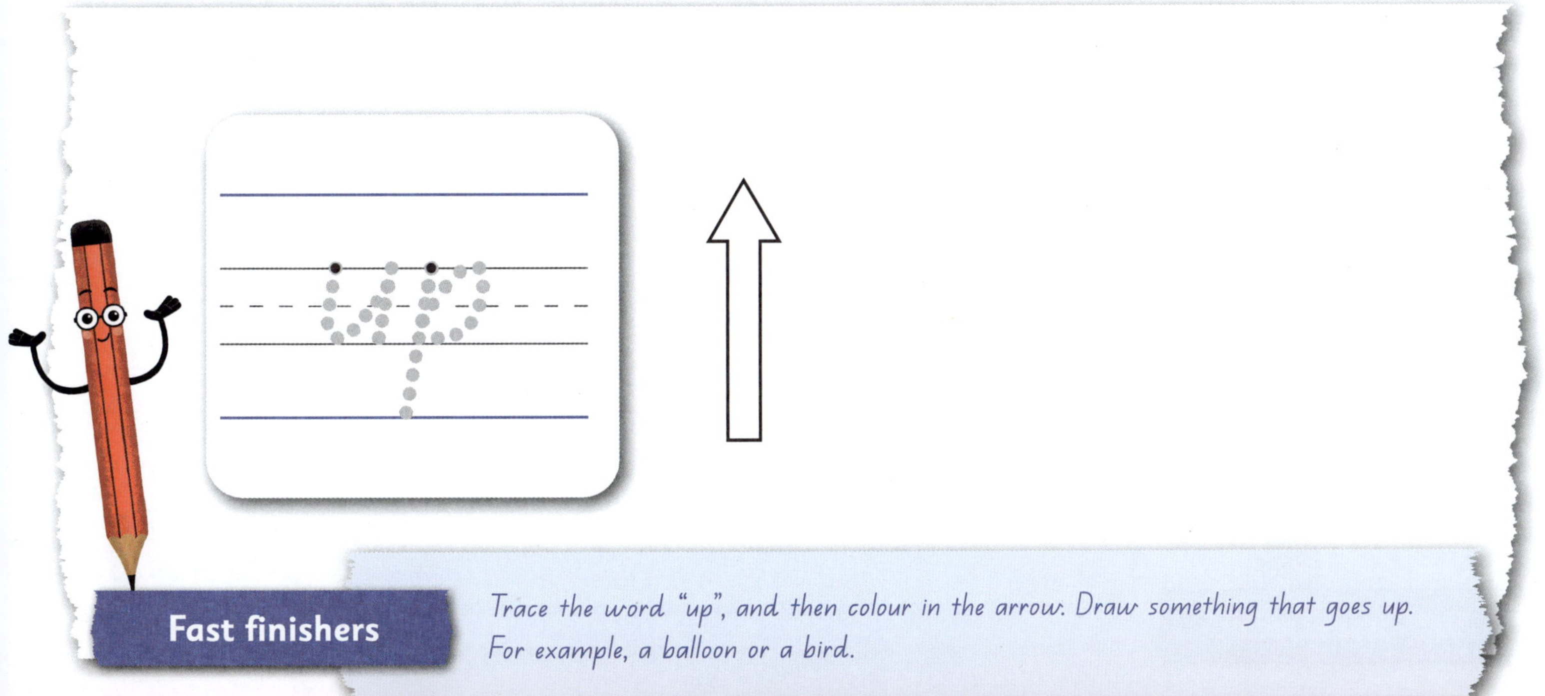

Fast finishers

Trace the word "up", and then colour in the arrow. Draw something that goes up. For example, a balloon or a bird.

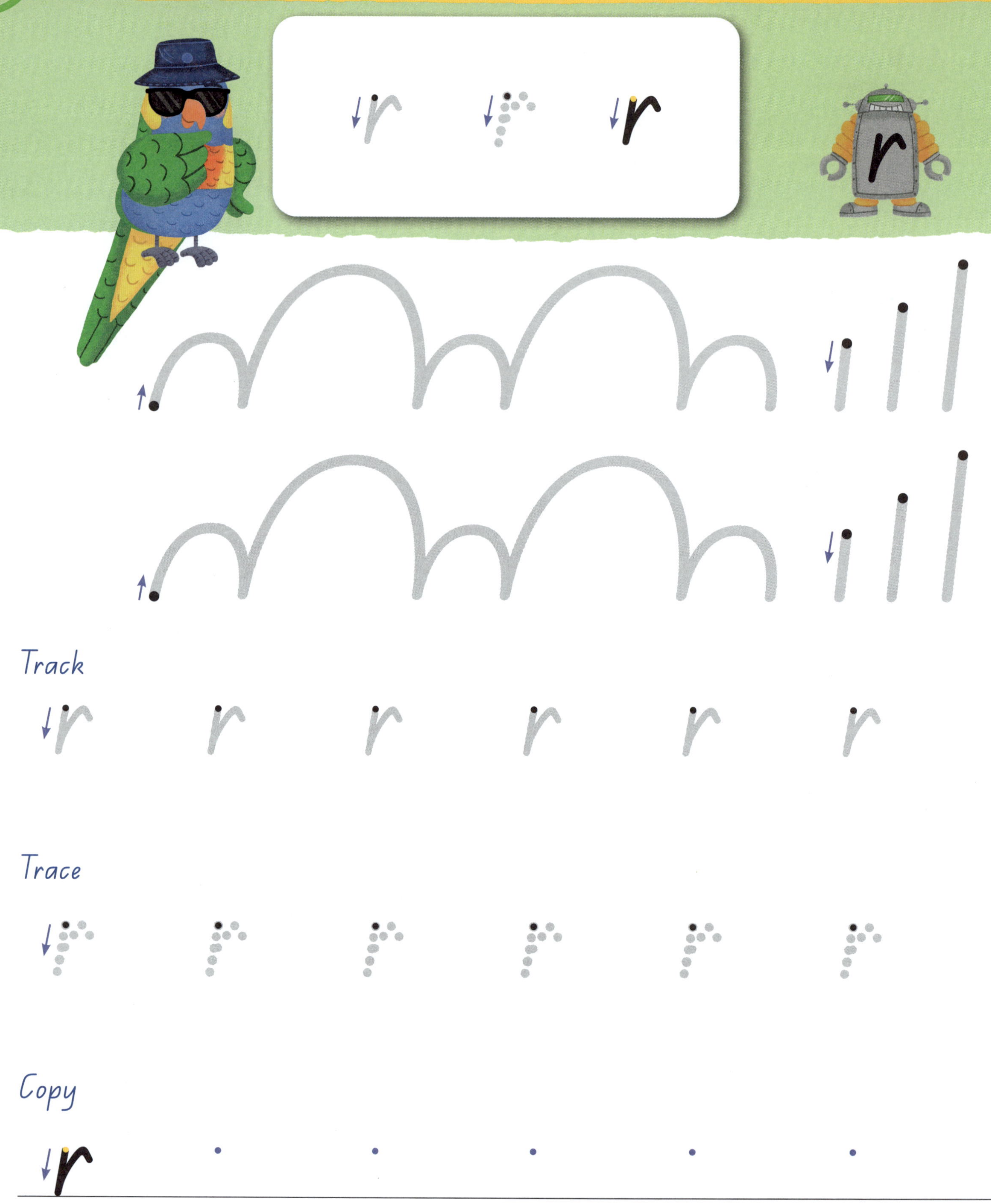

Self-assessment!

Ask students to circle their best lower-case r and upper-case R. Ask them to explain the reason for their choices to you or a classmate.

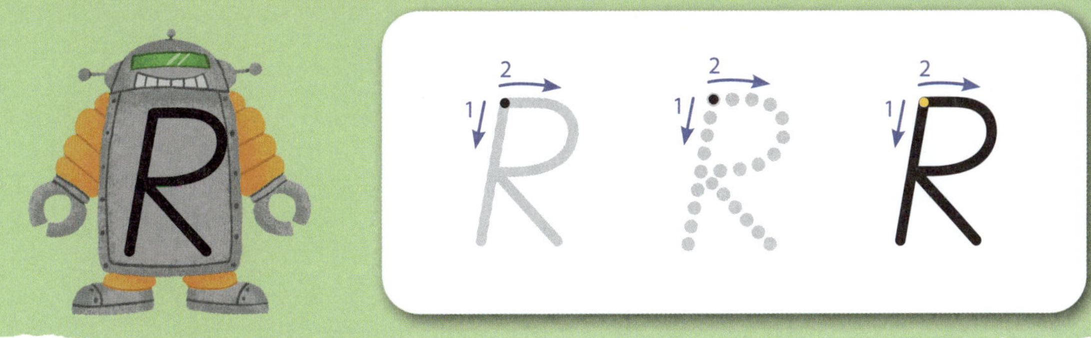

1 2 R
above
on
below

R
above
on
below

r
above
on
below

r
above
on
below

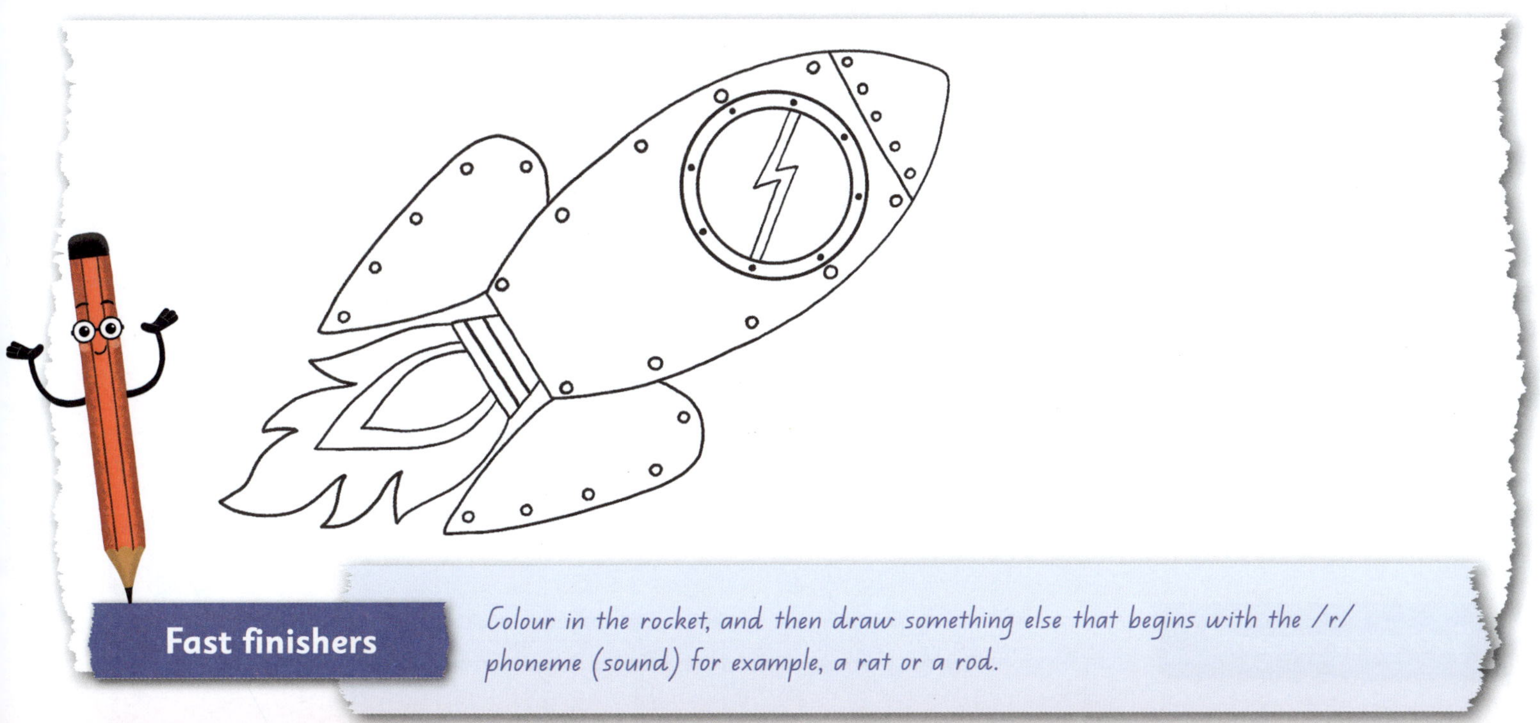

Fast finishers

Colour in the rocket, and then draw something else that begins with the /r/ phoneme (sound) for example, a rat or a rod.

Track

Trace

Copy

Self-assessment!

Ask students to circle their best lower-case h and upper-case H.
Ask them to explain the reason for their choices to you or a classmate.

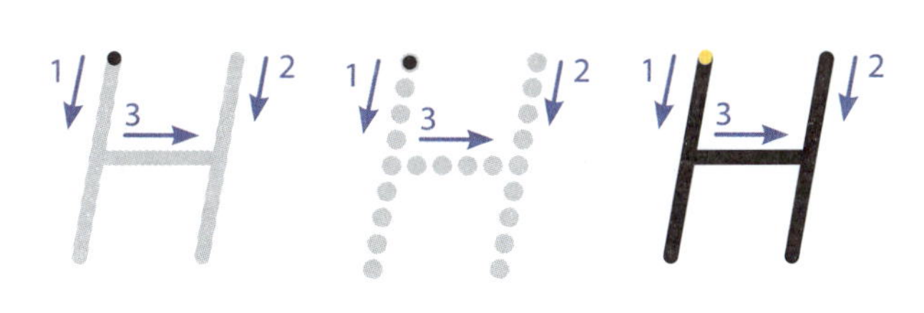

above
on
below

above
on
below

above
on
below

above
on
below

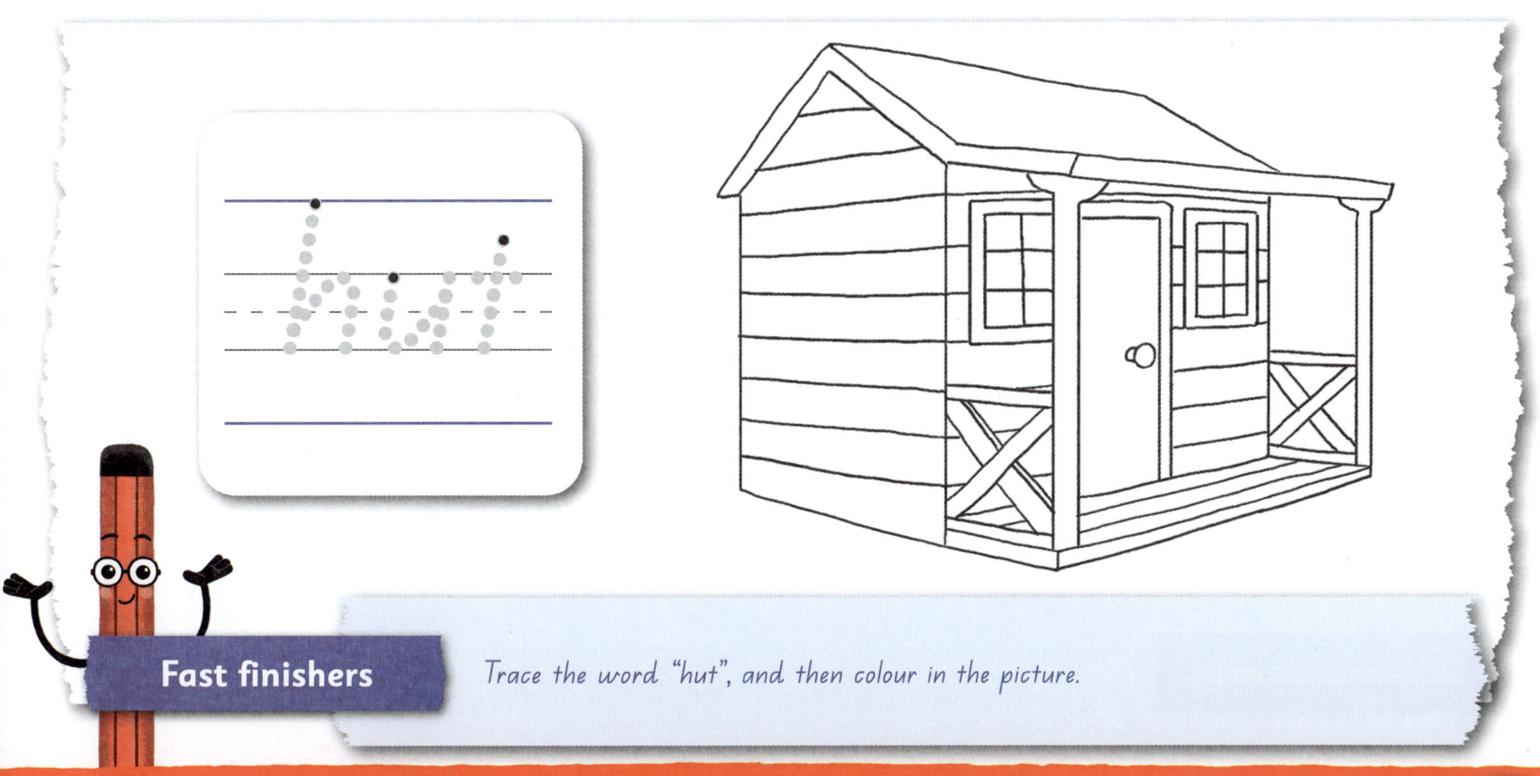

Fast finishers

Trace the word "hut", and then colour in the picture.

Track

b b b b b b

Trace

b b b b b b

Copy

b

Self-assessment!

Ask students to circle their best lower-case b and upper-case B. Ask them to explain the reason for their choices to you or a classmate.

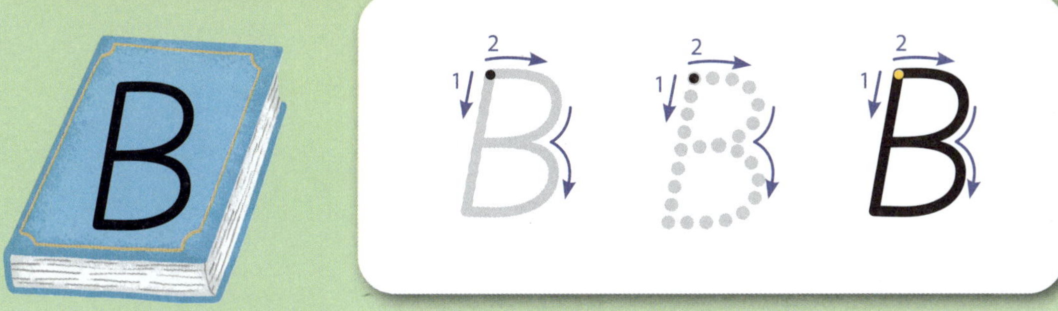

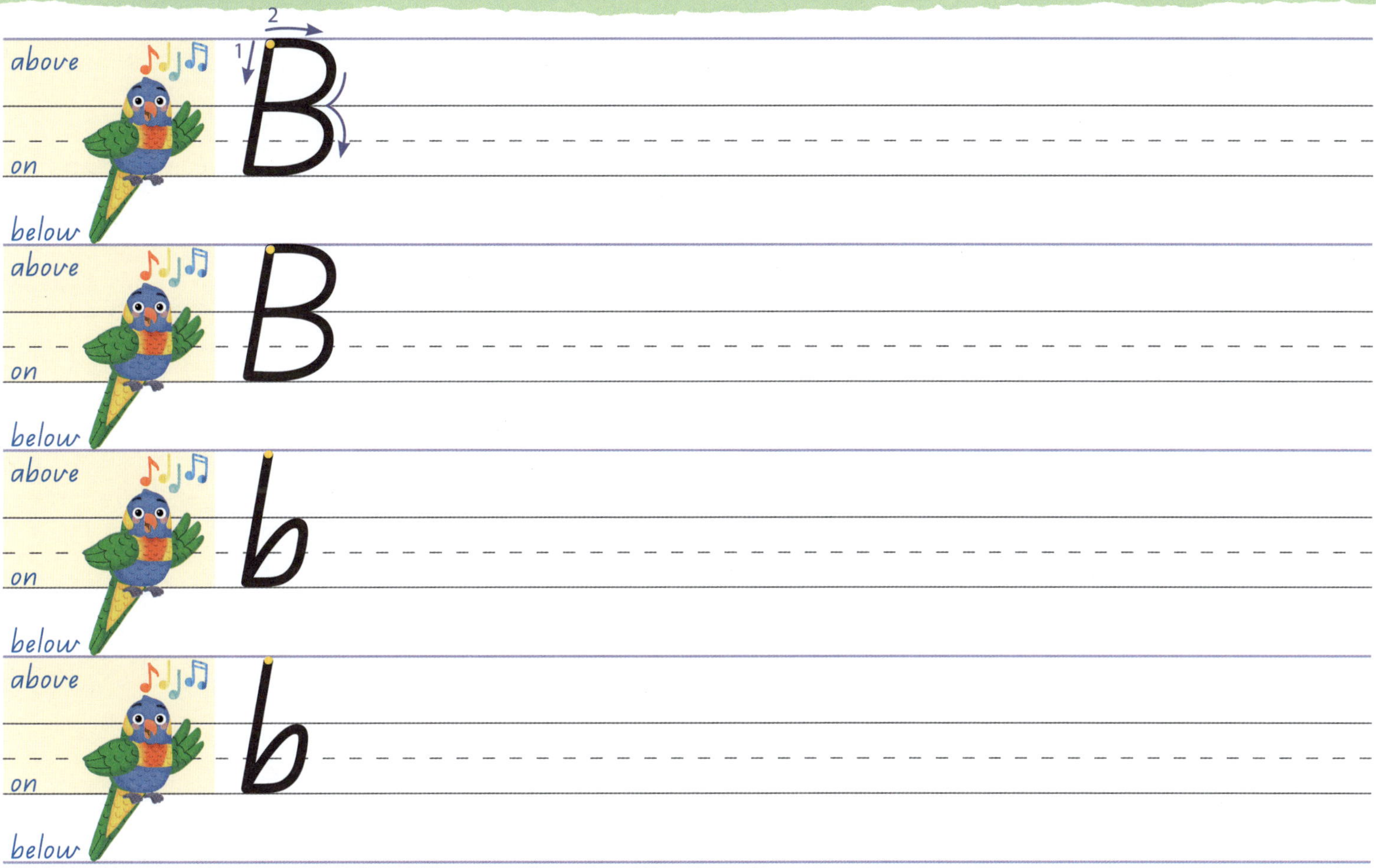

B

1
2
1
2
1
2

above
on
below
1
2
B
above
on
below
B
above
on
below
b
above
on
below
b

B
c
a
b
B
g
H
b
N

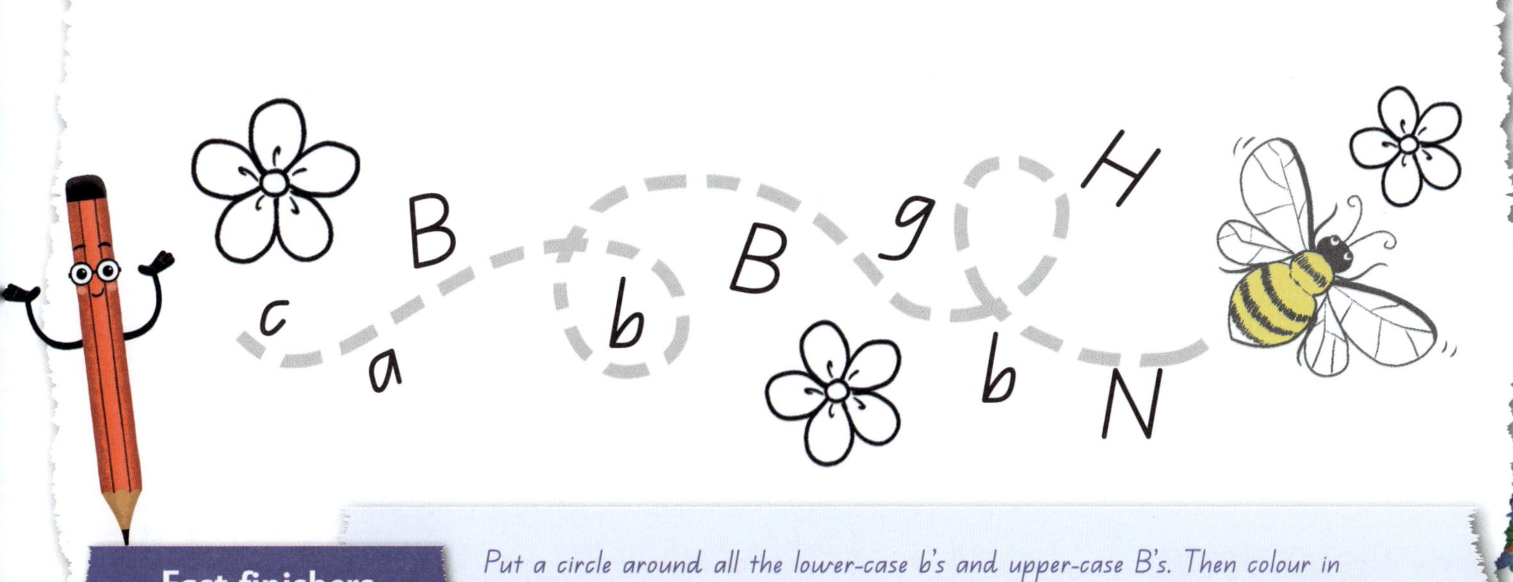

Fast finishers

Put a circle around all the lower-case b's and upper-case B's. Then colour in the flowers.

Track

Trace

Copy

Self-assessment!

Ask students to circle their best lower-case f and upper-case F.
Ask them to explain the reason for their choices to you or a classmate.

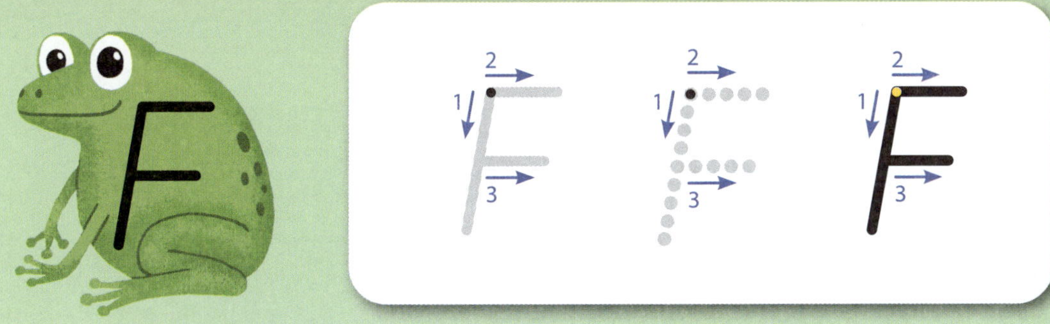

above

on

below

above

on

below

above

on

below

above

on

below

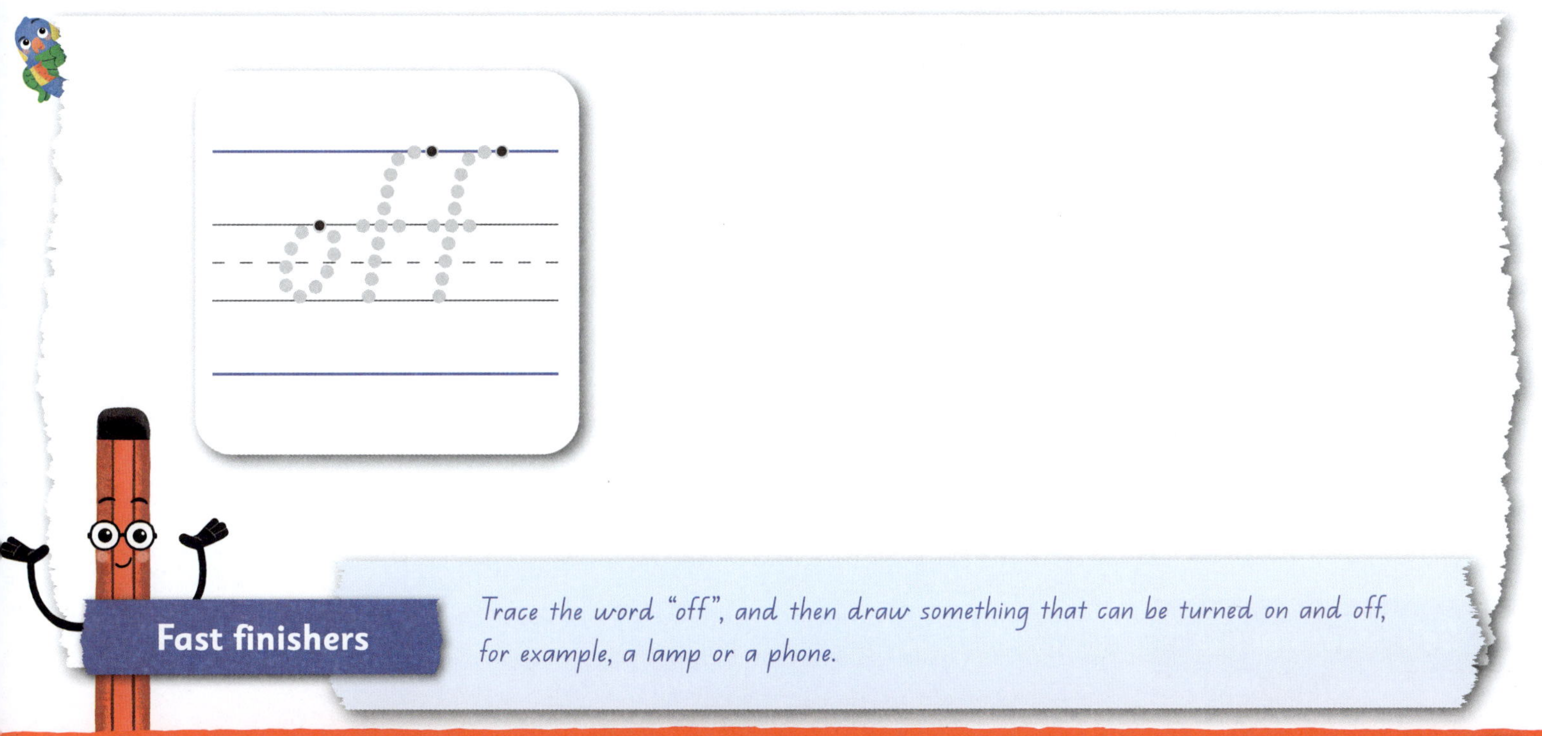

Fast finishers

Trace the word "off", and then draw something that can be turned on and off, for example, a lamp or a phone.

Track

Trace

Copy

Self-assessment!

Ask students to circle their best lower-case l and upper-case L.
Ask them to explain the reason for their choices to you or a classmate.

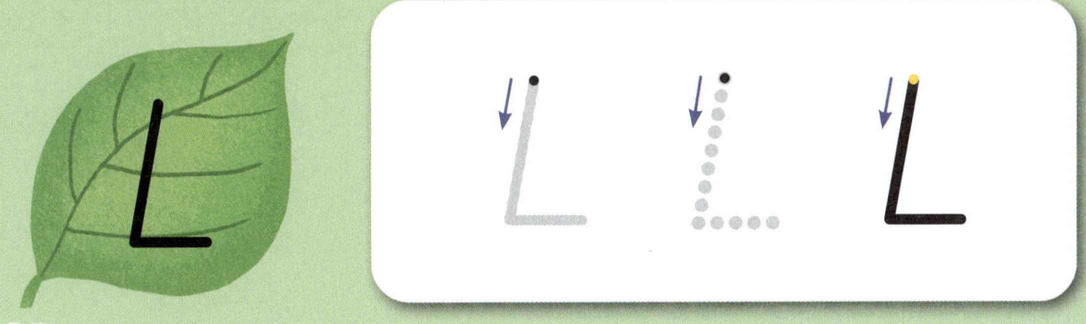

L L L

above
on
below
L

above
on
below
L

above
on
below
l

above
on
below
l

legs

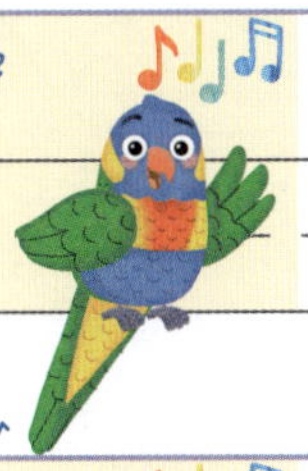

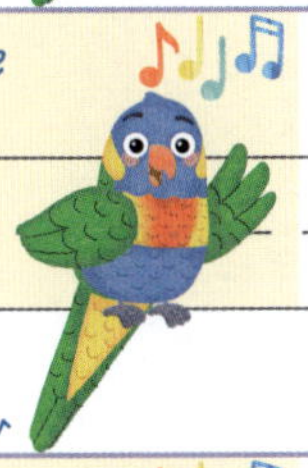

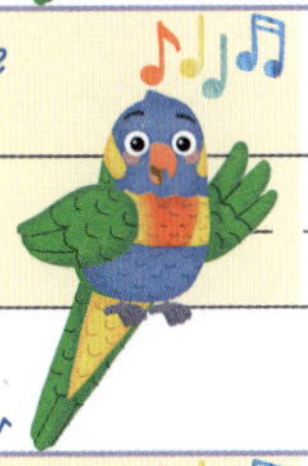

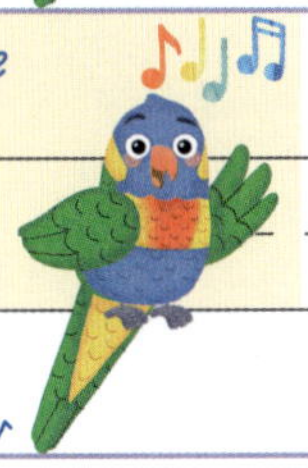

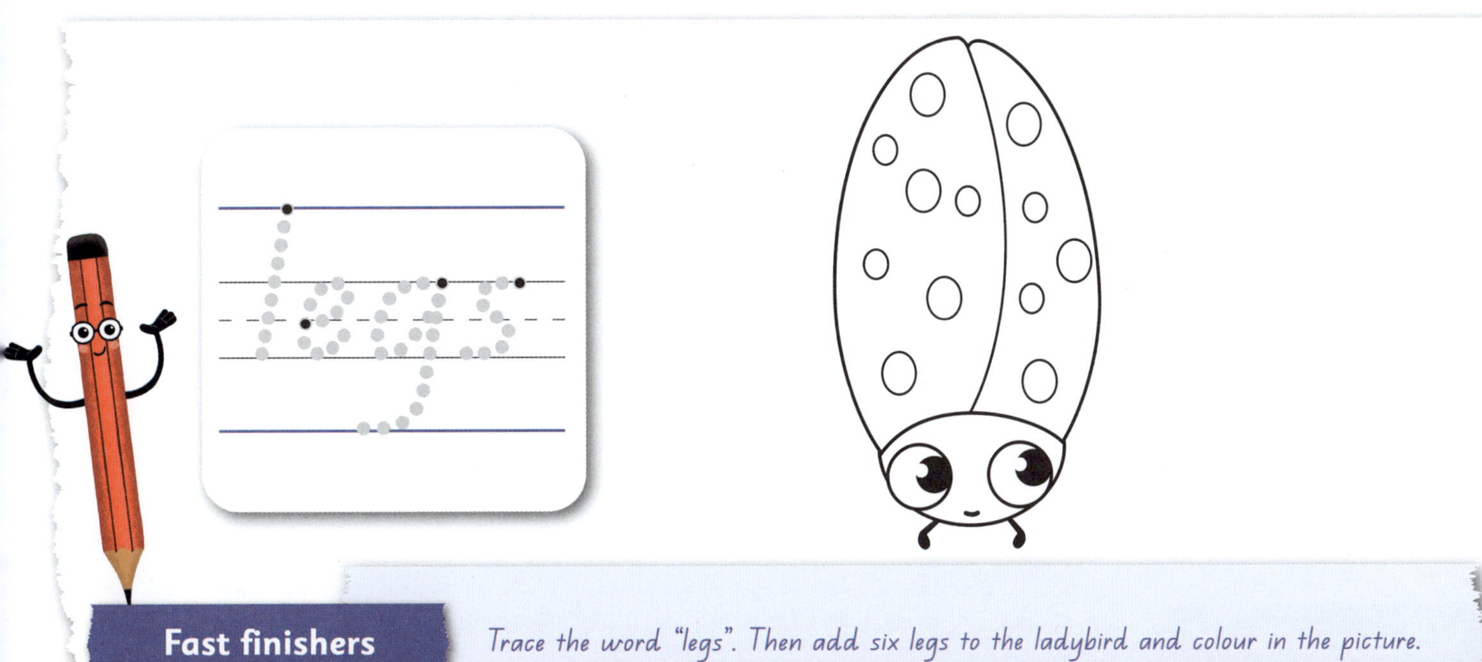

Fast finishers

Trace the word "legs". Then add six legs to the ladybird and colour in the picture.

Track

Trace

Copy

Self-assessment!

Ask students to circle their best lower-case j and upper-case J. Ask them to explain the reason for their choices to you or a classmate.

2
1
2
1
2
1

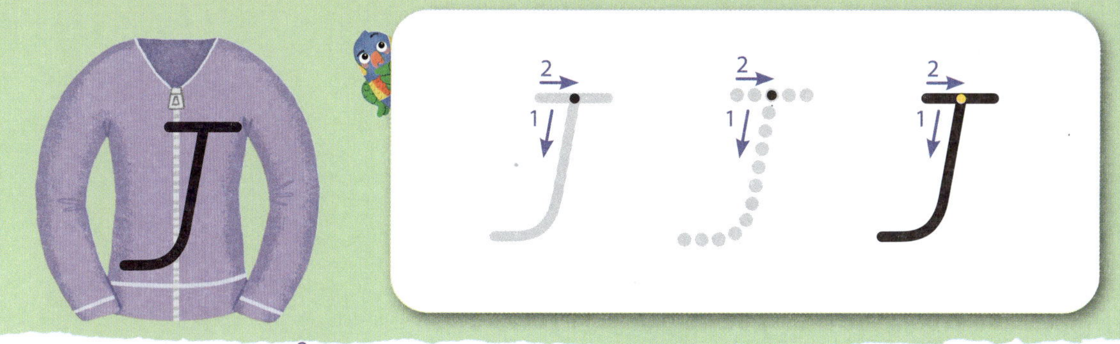

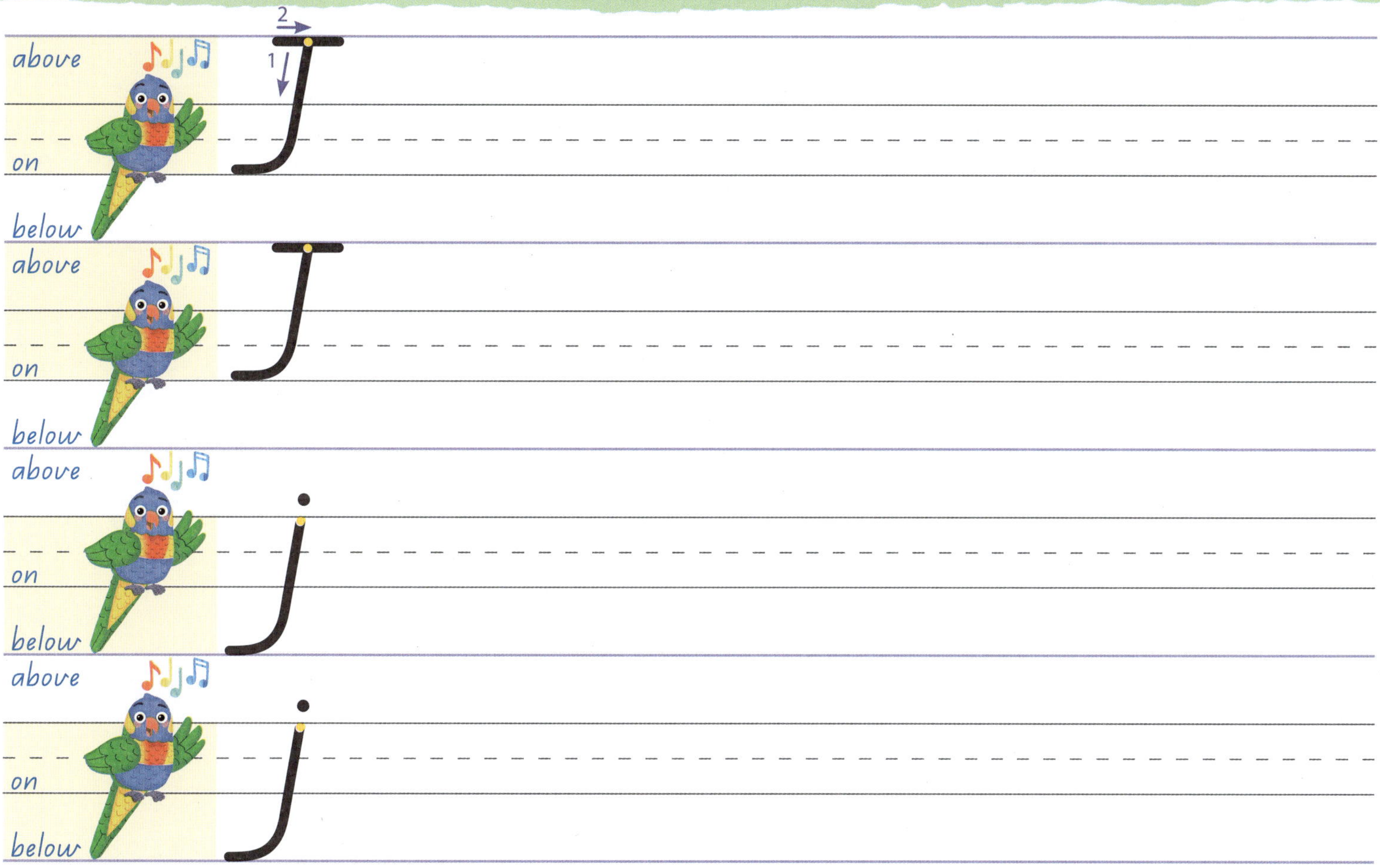

above
on
below
above
on
below
above
on
below
above
on
below

j
a
j
h
l

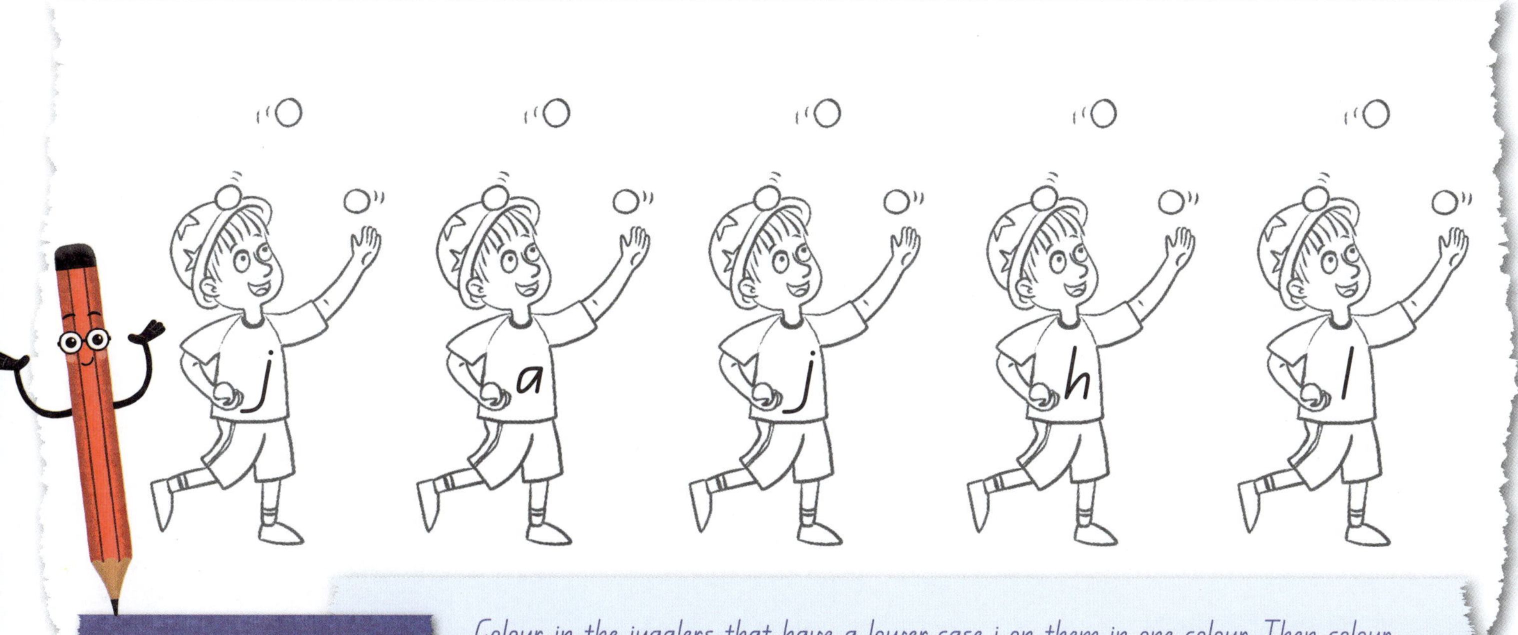

Fast finishers

Colour in the jugglers that have a lower-case j on them in one colour. Then colour the remaining jugglers in different colours.

Track

Trace

Copy

Self-assessment!

Ask students to circle their best lower-case v and upper-case V.
Ask them to explain the reason for their choices to you or a classmate.

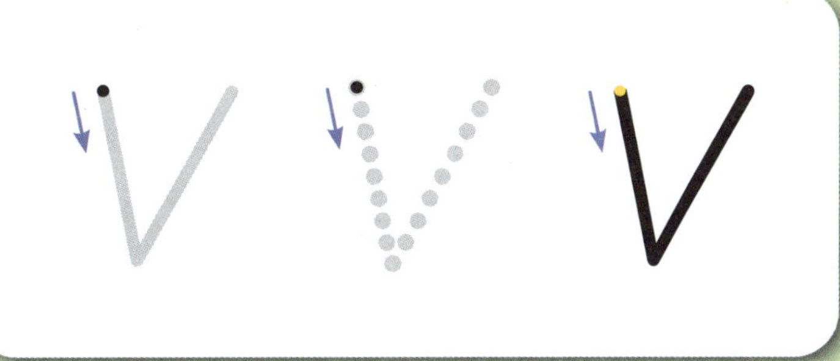

above
on
below

above
on
below

above
on
below

above
on
below

Fast finishers

Draw a picture of your favourite vegetable, and then colour it in.

Track

Trace

Copy

Self-assessment!

Ask students to circle their best lower-case w and upper-case W. Ask them to explain the reason for their choices to you or a classmate.

above
W
on
below

above
W
on
below

above
w
on
below

above
w
on
below

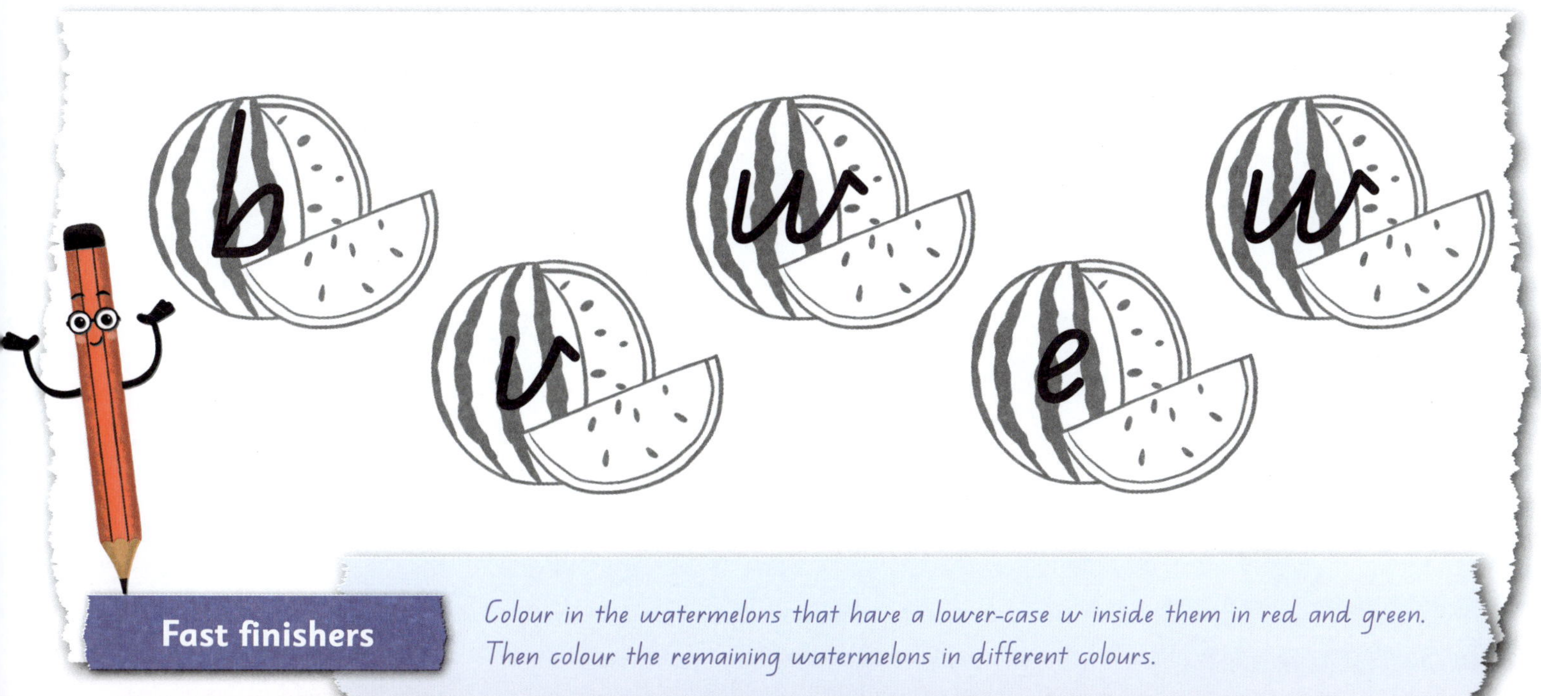

Fast finishers

Colour in the watermelons that have a lower-case w inside them in red and green. Then colour the remaining watermelons in different colours.

Trace

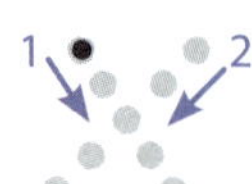     

Copy

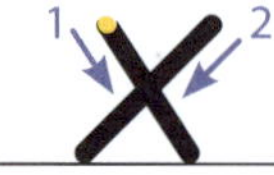

Self-assessment!

Ask students to circle their best lower-case x and upper-case X.
Ask them to explain the reason for their choices to you or a classmate.

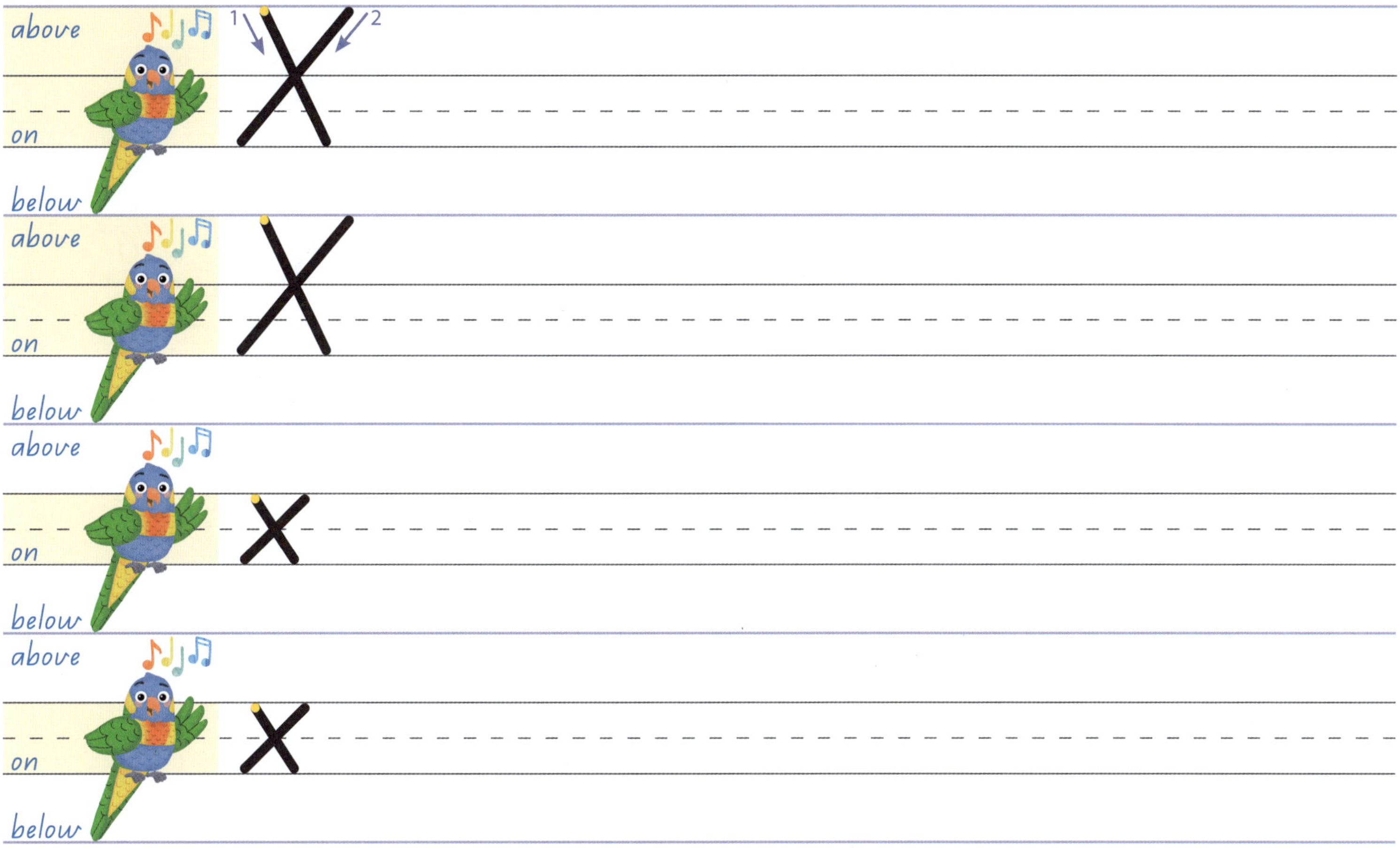

above
on
below

above
on
below

above
on
below

above
on
below

Fast finishers

Trace the word "six", and then draw six things. For example, six faces, six bugs or six cups.

Track

Trace

Copy

Self-assessment!

Ask students to circle their best lower-case y and upper-case Y.
Ask them to explain the reason for their choices to you or a classmate.

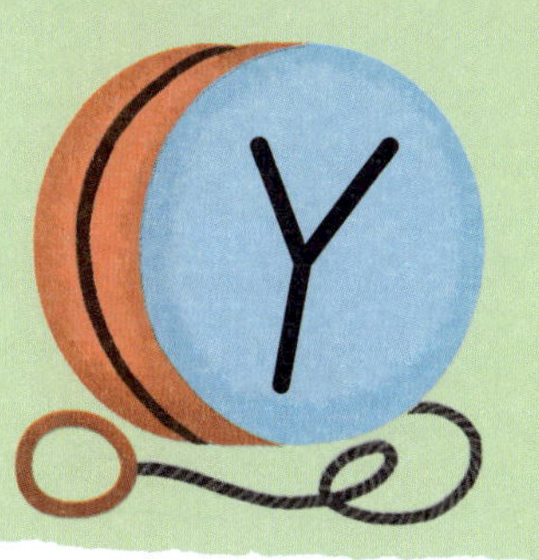

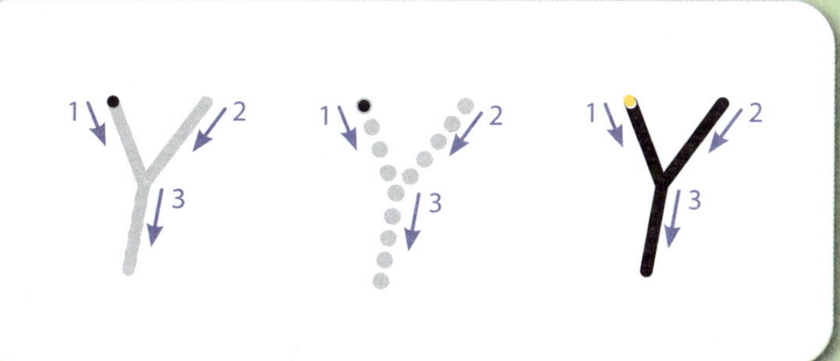

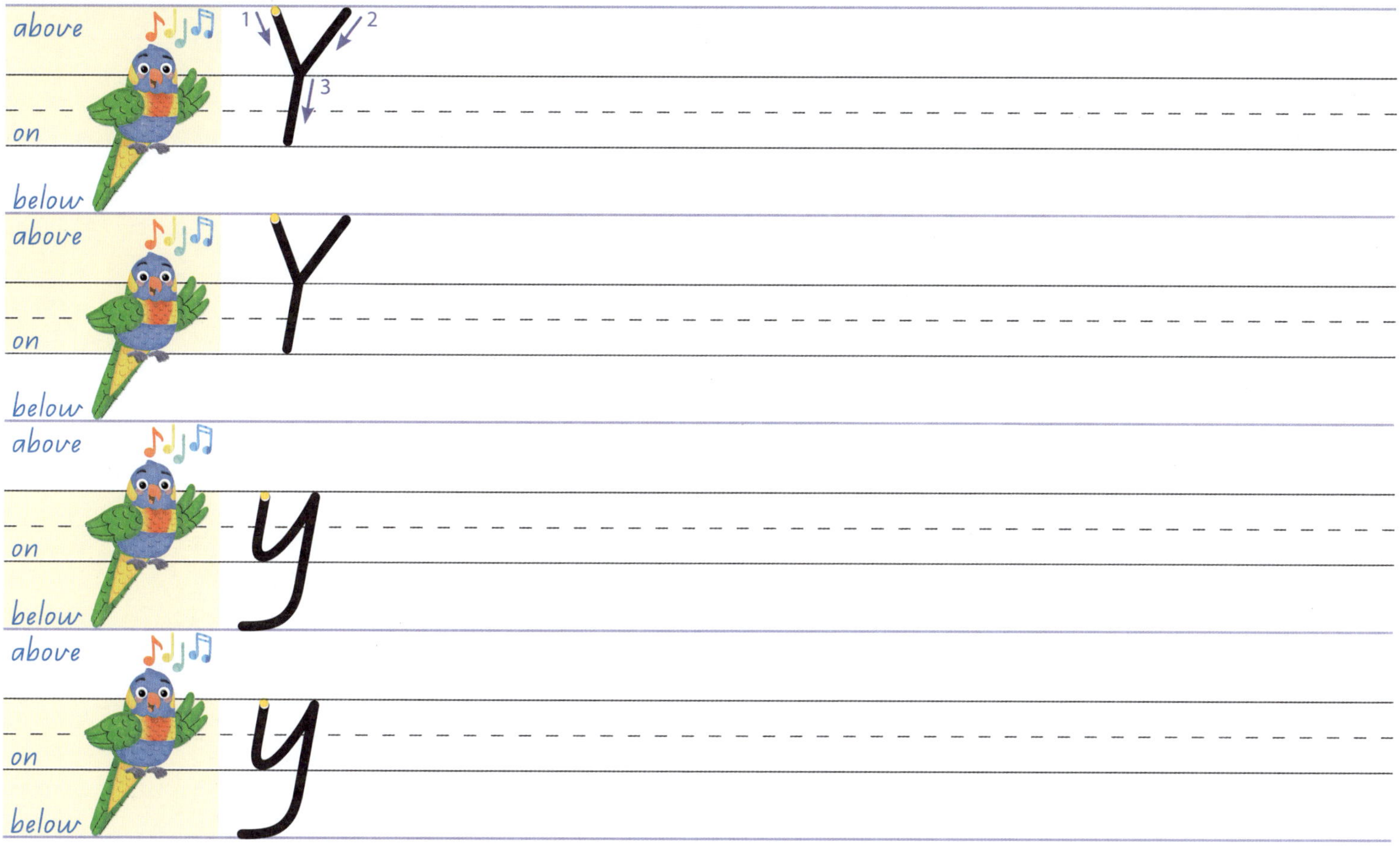

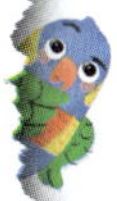

Y

1 2 3
1 2 3
1 2 3

above
on
below
1 Y 2 3
above
on
below
Y
above
on
below
y
above
on
below
y

h Y y Y y f
w c e a

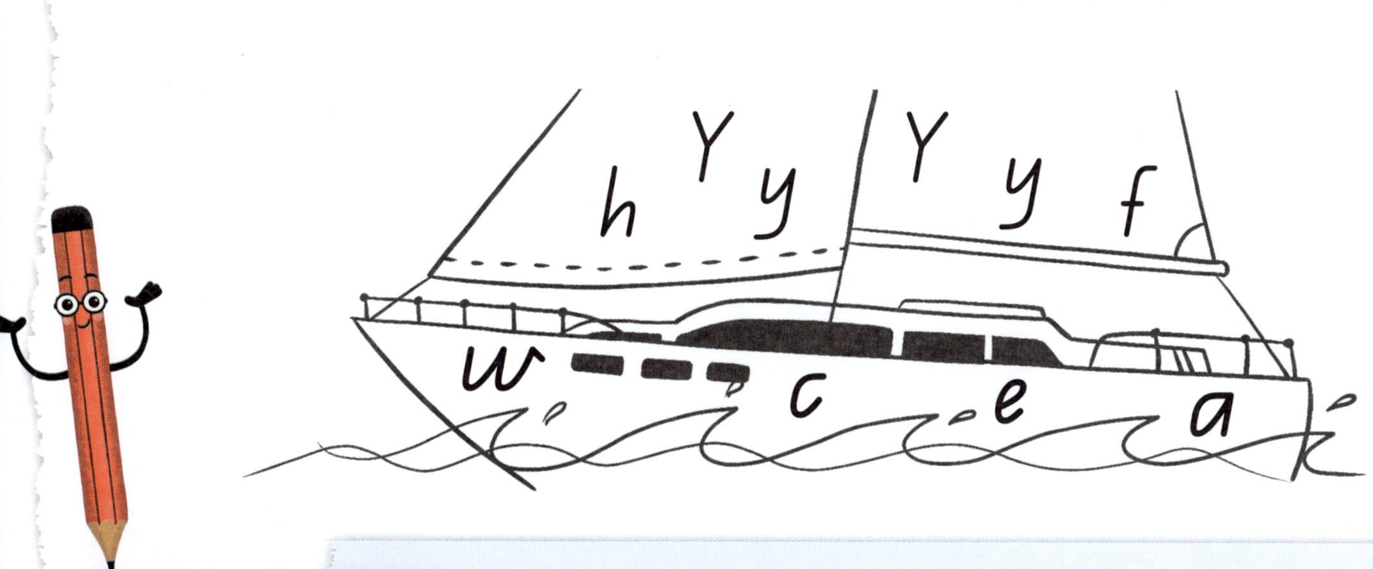

Fast finishers

Circle all the lower-case y's and upper-case Y's. What could you add to this picture? For example, a bird, the Sun or a fish. What could you colour in yellow?

Track

z z z z z z

Trace

z z z z z z

Copy

z

Self-assessment!

Ask students to circle their best lower-case z and upper-case Z. Ask them to explain the reason for their choices to you or a classmate.

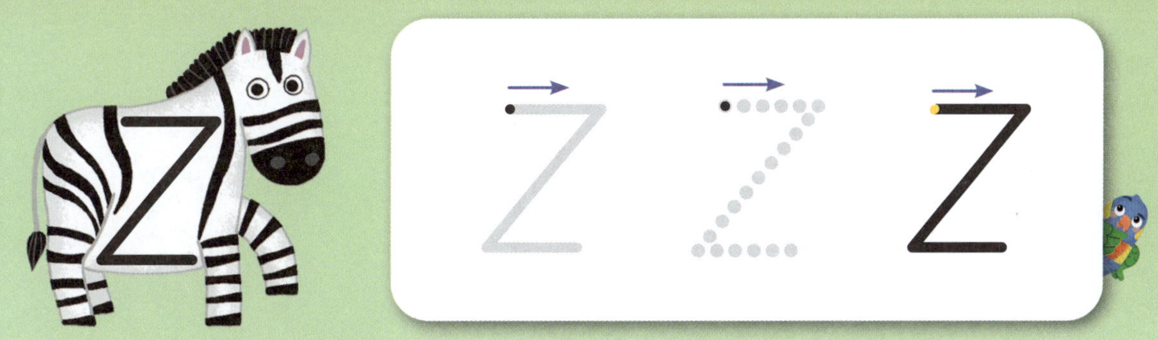

Z Z Z

above

on

below

Z

above

on

below

Z

above

on

below

z

above

on

below

z

zoo

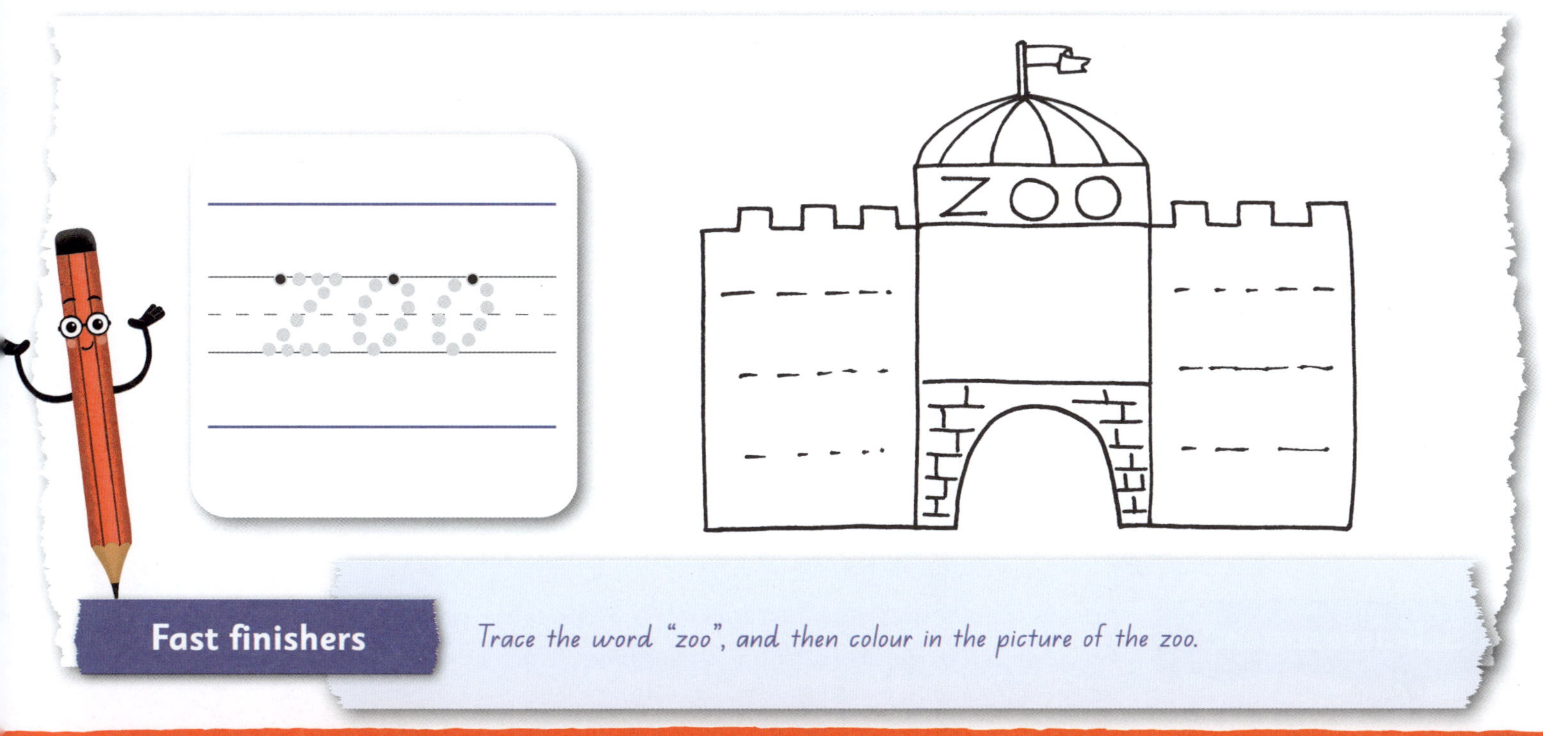

Fast finishers

Trace the word "zoo", and then colour in the picture of the zoo.

Track

Trace

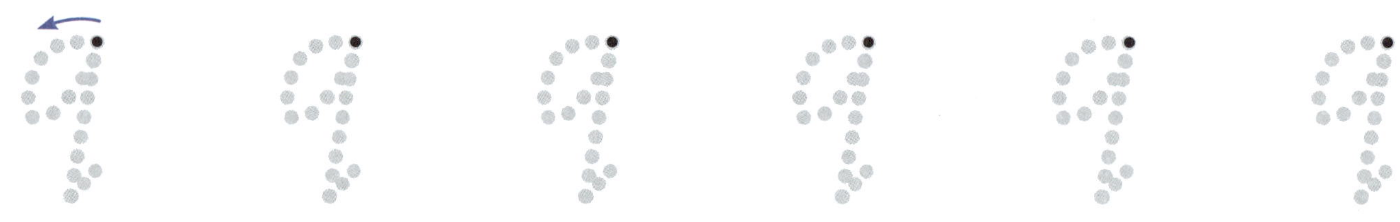

Copy

Self-assessment!

Ask students to circle their best lower-case q and upper-case Q.
Ask them to explain the reason for their choices to you or a classmate.

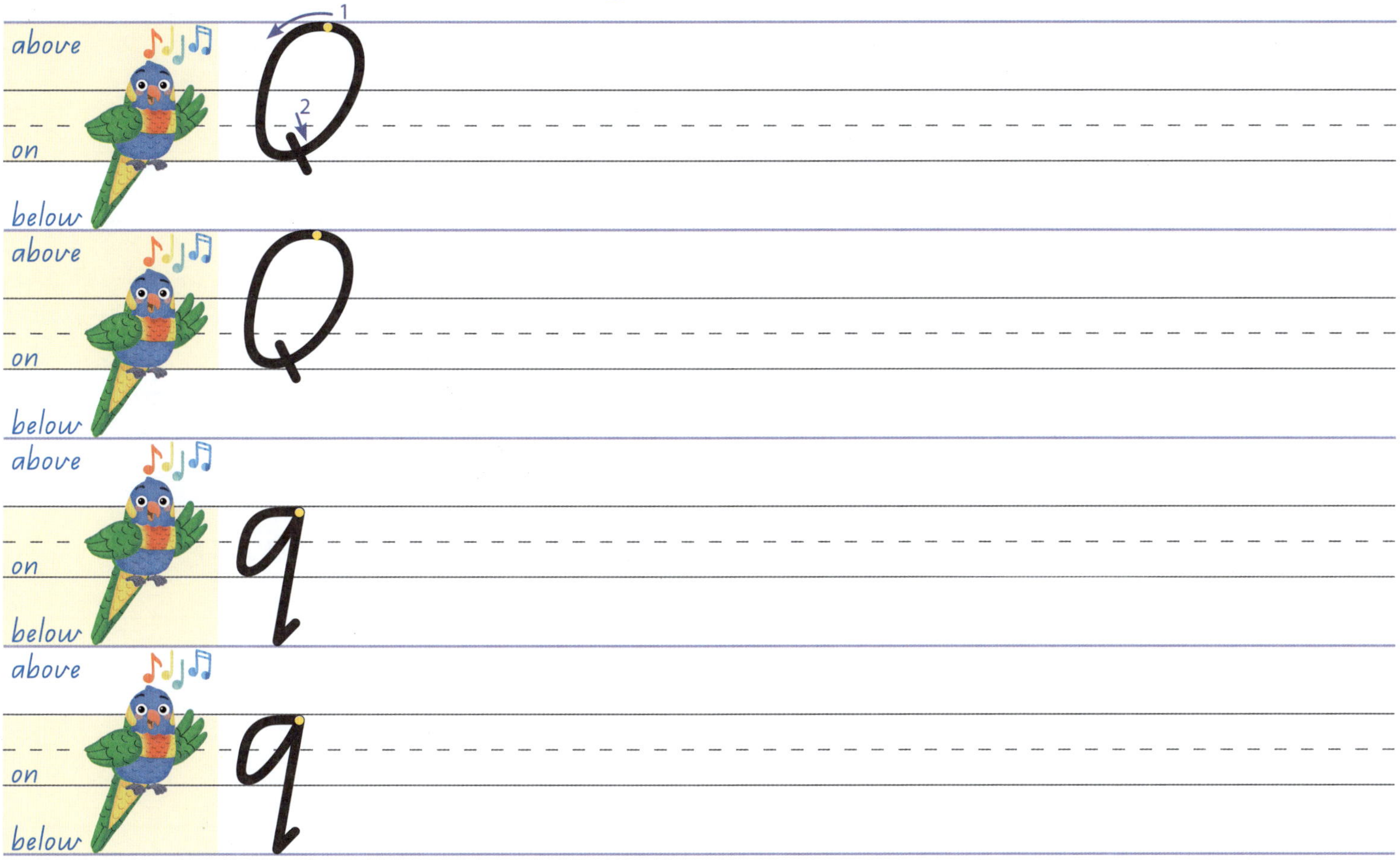

above
on
below

above
on
below

above
on
below

above
on
below

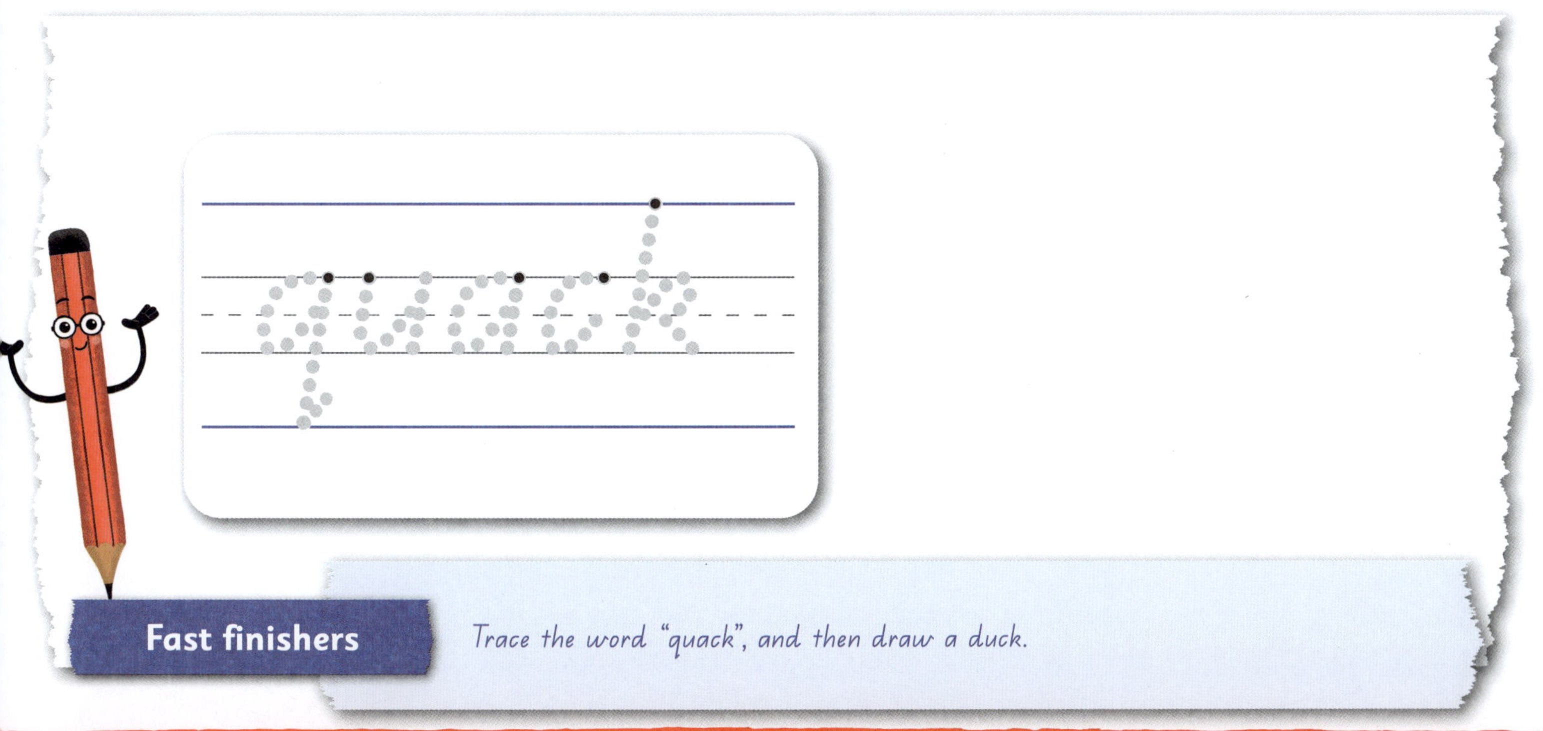

Fast finishers Trace the word "quack", and then draw a duck.

Number practice

Track, trace and copy the numbers.

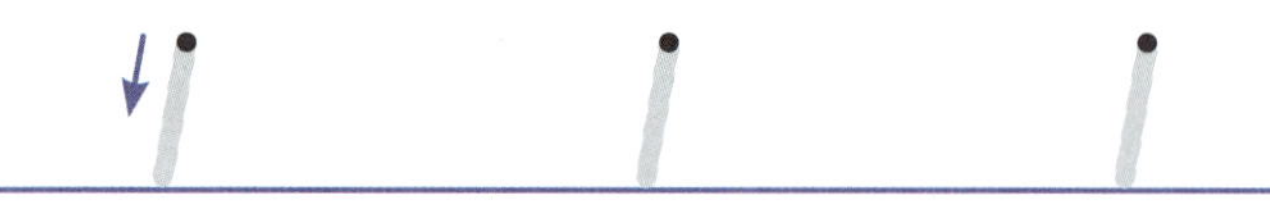

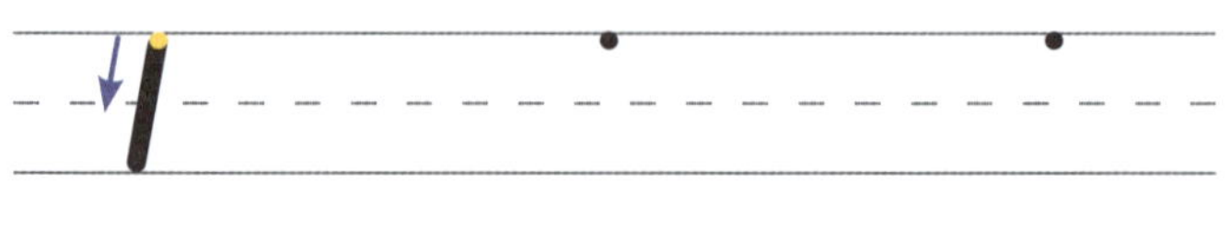

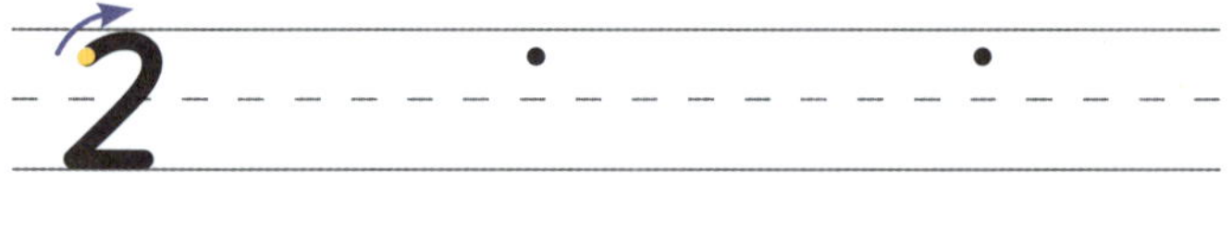

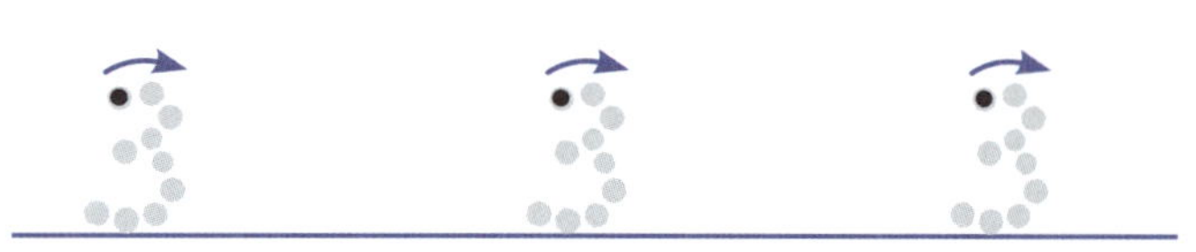

1 4 2 4 4

1 2 1 2 1 2

4 1 2

2 1 5 5 5

2 1 2 1 2 1

5 2 1

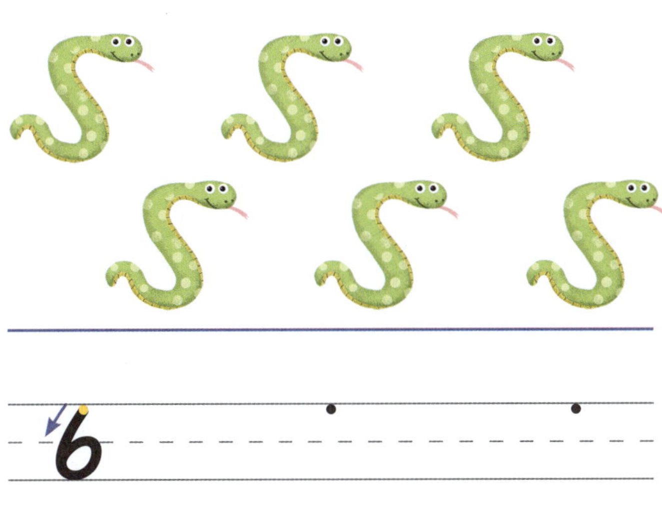

6 6 6

6

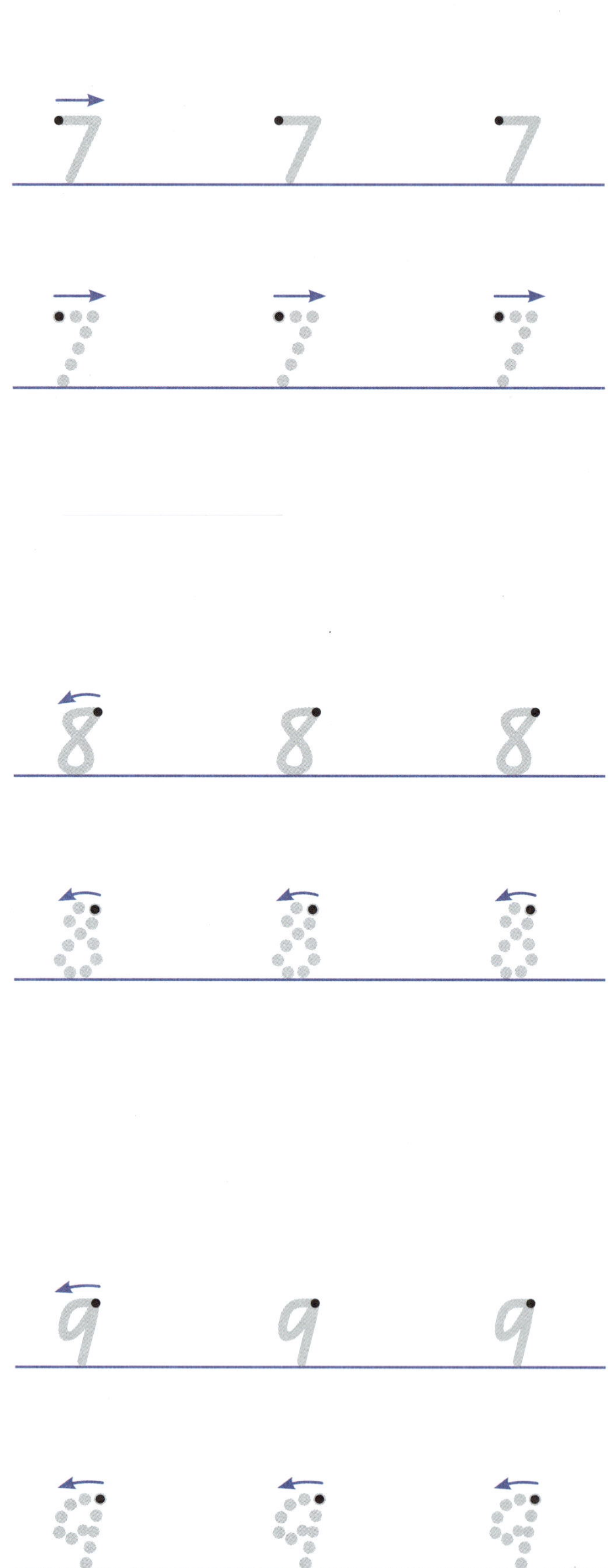

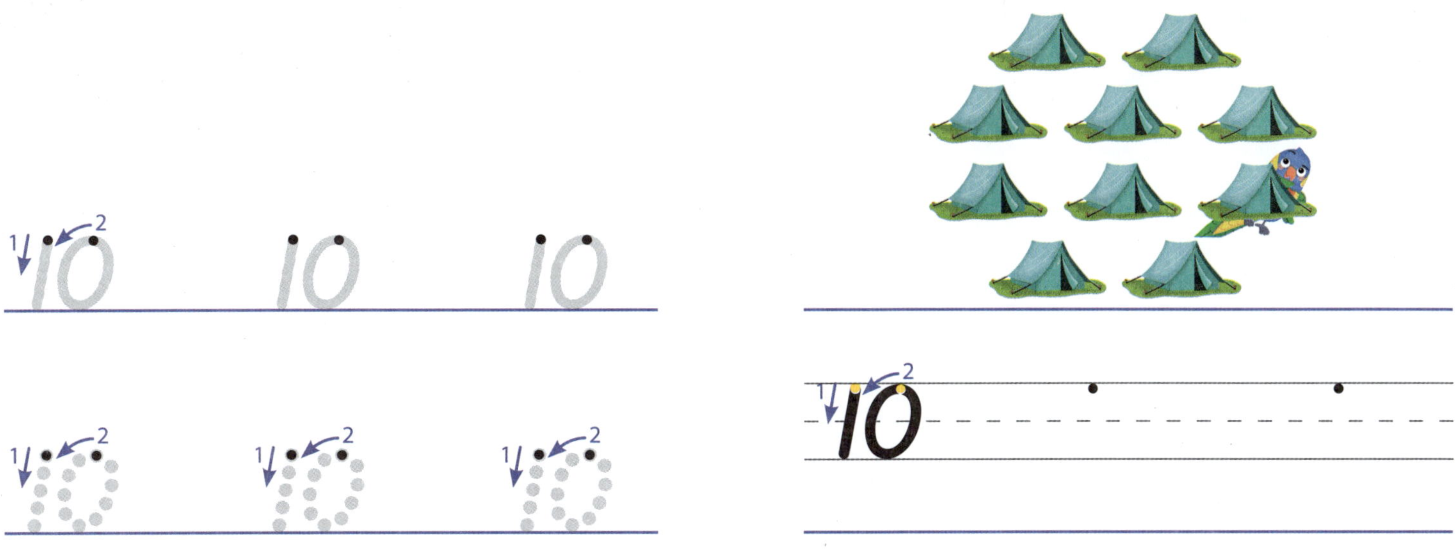

Fast finishers *Choose your favourite number, and then draw a picture with that number of animals.*

Alphabet

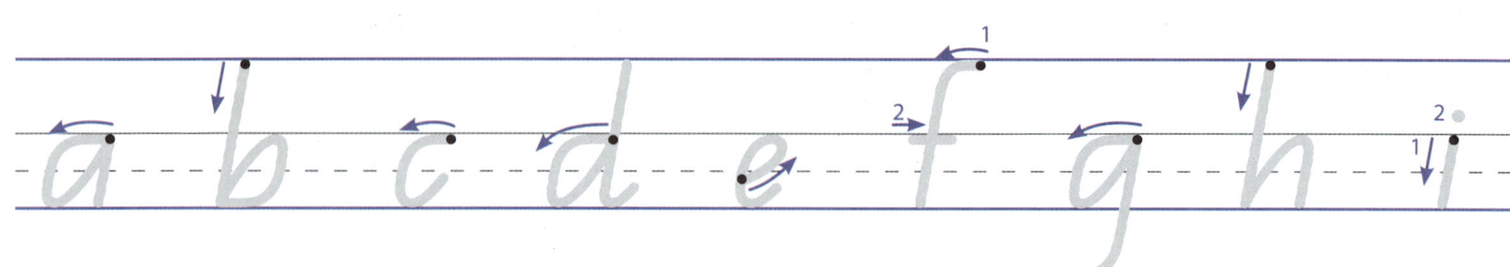

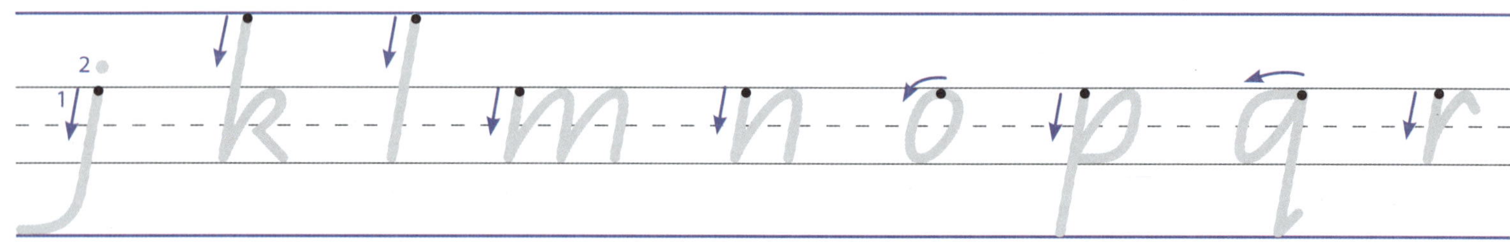

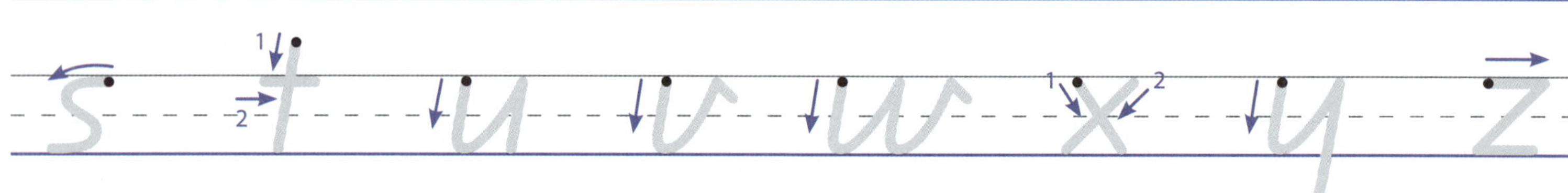

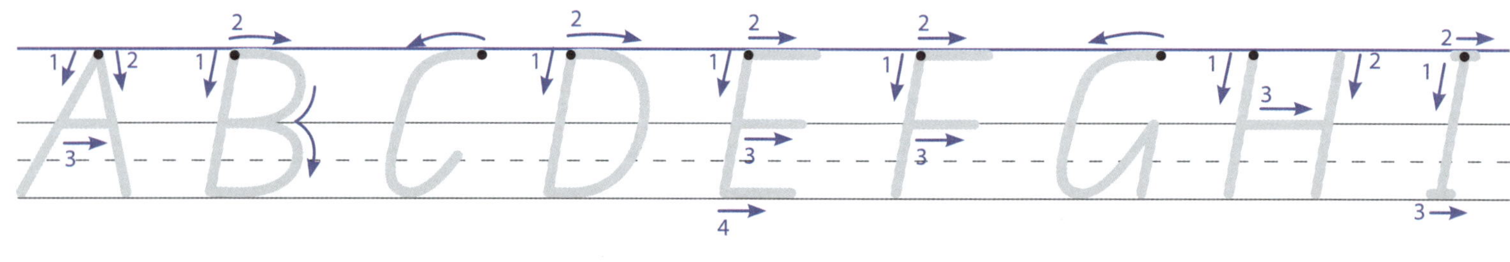

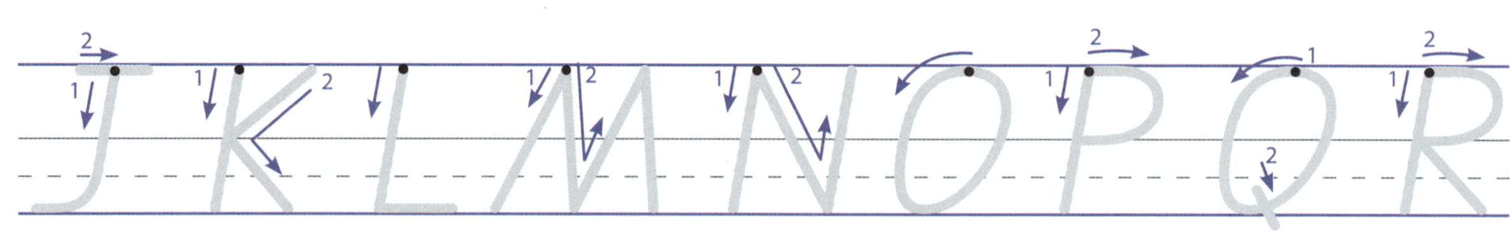

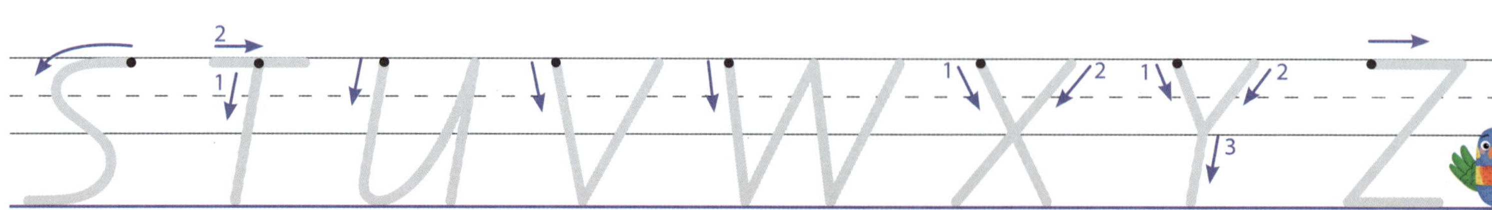